A Voice in the Wilderness, volume 6

Watchman, What of the Night?

Dalen Garris

This is a work of history. Historical individuals and places and events are mentioned.

Published by Revivalfire Ministries

ISBN 13: 978-1-7342213-6-7

All Scripture is from the King James Version

For information, address
dale@revivalfire.org

First paperback printing January, 2021

Printed in the United States of America

Rev. 2.1

The burden of Dumah.

He calleth to me out of Seir, Watchman, what of the night? Watchman, what of the night?

The watchman said, The morning cometh, and also the night: if ye will enquire, enquire ye: return, come.

(Isaiah 21:11-12)

Table of Contents

Babel

"And they said, Go to, let us build us a city and a tower, whose top may reach unto heaven; and let us make us a name, lest we be scattered abroad upon the face of the whole earth." Genesis 11:4

I'm sure this sounded like a good idea to them at the time, but it didn't to God.

When Noah's little family had been dropped off onto the wide expanse of a newly cleansed Earth, you'd have thought that, with a fresh new beginning and a cataclysmic break with rampant sin, Noah's little group would have been tightly bound together. The fractious nature of man, however, introduced itself almost immediately with Noah's son, Ham, and drove a wedge of sin into this new foundation of mankind. Six hundred years later, they were scattered over the Earth with no clear direction, goal, or vision. Building a tower for unity must have sounded like a pretty good idea.

We are sheep – the Lord said so – and as sheep, we need someone to lead us, or we tend to wander off in mindless directions. Whenever there is a vacuum in leadership, there will be many who flock to all sorts of charlatans and will succumb to the charisma of self-appointed avatars. And so it was with Nimrod. It is the basis of all false religions.

That's why Jesus died – so we could have a personal relationship with our Savior and be led by God, not someone else.

But when God doesn't move as fast as we think He should, we get scared that He won't move at all. And since we know we are sheep, we are afraid we will end up dispersed with no cohesive focus to our existence. We have always had a hard time learning to trust God.

But God has a plan, even if we don't, and He expects us to do it His way, not ours.

Unity in God is not built from the ground up but from Heaven down. While we prefer to appoint a commission to study the problem and come up with a solution, God likes to appoint yielded, broken vessels who will do it His way. And it is hardly ever the way that we would have chosen.

When we rely upon our own carnal efforts to build a tower to reach Heaven, all we will end up with is another religion. Only when we surrender and learn to wait upon God instead of trying to figure it out for ourselves will we find that unity with God.

Silence

"And when he had opened the seventh seal, there was silence in heaven about the space of half an hour." Revelation 8:1

Ominous words.

This is one of the most frightening scriptures in the entire Bible. There is a certain awe of bated breath as you can feel the wrath of God welling up before being unleashed upon the Earth. This is not about to happen somewhere else at some other time to some other people -- this is about to fall upon us, here, and very possibly in this generation.

And yet, like children on a playground, we are too busy playing to give much thought to what may be coming. Even when we see the cumulous clouds begin to build and darken on the horizon, it is still sunny here, and we are not yet concerned. Perhaps it will not rain yet today, or the storm will turn and hit somewhere else. Or it may not even rain at all. And even if it does, surely our Teacher and Guardian will call us in from the playground so that we will escape the downpour.

That is the same mentality that the Israelites had when Jerusalem was besieged by the Babylonian army. As the old prophet Isaiah related, they looked from their housetops and could see the danger over the wall, but with singing and dancing, they declared, "Let us eat and drink; for tomorrow we shall die" (Isa. 22:13). They never really thought that God would allow the enemy to break down the wall of Jerusalem and carry them away to Babylon.

But He did.

We have seen terrible storm clouds arise in our times, from 9/11 to one war after another. I have stated before that there will be three wars, and one war will roll into another until the big one comes that will decimate 1/3 of the population. It is coming, and we shall see it. And yet, we hope for peace in our time.

Natural holocausts have hit us, but we proclaim that we will build for tomorrow. Just an anomaly, we say, and nothing to worry about. God would never do anything like that to us. And yet it is written that He rules the winds and the waves.

The threat of worldwide pestilence hovers over us, but it is something that could never really happen here. We have modern medicine to protect us.

Solomon said that the words of wise men are heard in quiet more than the cry of him that ruleth among fools (Eccl. 9:17). And so it is today. We would rather sing and dance on our housetops while we view the danger beyond the city walls than listen to the warnings that cry for repentance and a soul searching for our churches. The sun is still shining, and we still have time to play. Surely no harm will come to us.

The old prophet saw this same thing and heard a word to cry out a warning. In his frustration, he called out, "What shall I cry?" They have heard, they have seen, but they will not hearken to the call for repentance. And the answer comes back that all flesh will fade away like the grass of the field, but the Word of the Lord will surely come to pass (Isa. 40:6). And so, we cry, but our warnings are drowned out by the cry of those who rule among fools.

But in the distance can be heard the drum roll and the cadence of marching feet approaching ever so surely.

Quietness

Have you ever been out in the middle of a calm sea with no wind or waves to break the monotony? The circle of the horizon offers no points of distinction, and the calm, still air smothers any sense of direction. You sit still in a boat without oars as you feel time dissolve around you. With no place to go and no way to get there, you find yourself in a situation where you have to yield to the suppression of your spirit as even the air itself smothers you into silence.

There are times in your Christian walk that God will bring you into such a solitary place. It is not only a time for reflection but also for the quieting of your own spirit. It is one of the toughest experiences that you will ever have to go through in God, but when He places you there, you have no choice but to sit still and wait.

All the great personalities in the Word of God went through times like that before they were called into the thick of what would become the real essence of their ministry. Abraham had his walk through the land of Canaan, never understanding where he was going or why. Moses had his 40 years on the backside of the desert. Joseph cooled his heels in prison, forgotten by everyone for 13 years. Elijah did his time in the desert, as did Paul and Jesus. Jonah only spent 3 days in the belly of a whale, but I'm sure he would have traded that with Moses' 40 years in a heartbeat.

When we begin our journey in life to serve the Lord, we often rush headlong in zeal and excitement to accomplish the great things that we feel are set before us. We charge off on our white stallion to conquer the forces of darkness and set the captives free. The rush of the wind blowing through our hair as we hold up the Blood-Stained Banner in a galloping charge is exhilarating. The thrill of victory runs through us as we battle through one enemy after another.

But then the time comes when we find ourselves in that quiet place, and the adrenaline that was pumping through our veins drains out of us, leaving us frantic in the midst of the calm. While we fret about being abandoned and left out to pasture, we wonder what we did wrong.

Has God forsaken us for someone else? It feels like being left by a faithless lover for someone who is younger and better looking. Satan is right there at our shoulder to confirm all this. He whispers to us that we're finished, washed up, and God is done with us. It is hard not to despair when all around you, others are charging off into their own victories with that same look of conquest on their faces that you had at one time.

If God would just set us down and explain to us what is going on, this would be easy. But then, that's the whole point – it isn't supposed to be easy. Battles are easy because at least you know what is going on, but sitting in the midst of this barren desert is killing you. Common sense and carnal reasoning cry that this is a mistake – God should be using you in some strong way, especially since you have proven yourself so faithful in all that you have fought for. You have done everything He has asked of you, so why has He dropped you off into a place of nothingness?

These are the times that break your spirit and take the "you" out of "you." You are left with nothing that remains of the great Christian warrior you saw yourself as. Your strength is drained, and you are left with only one thing – hope. Not hope in your victories or your accomplishments, but with hope in that faint glimmer that leads to the mercy of God. Nothing else matters.

No matter how many miracles Jesus did, no matter how many dead He raised, no matter how many sermons He delivered, it was not until He was completely broken on that Old Rugged Cross and had surrendered His life to death that the greatest victory of all time was won.

Only when you have reached that same broken, crucified rest on the Cross will your victory also be complete.

Apostles

What is an Apostle? The whole idea of an apostle carries a hefty weight with it, but just exactly what is an apostle?

Technically, an apostle is someone who is sent with a commission from God, like an envoy, but with more authority than just a missionary or a preacher. This is someone with an anointing of authority that comes directly from the Throne of God, and as such, the words that they speak carry the weight of a spiritual authority that supersedes any ecclesiastical rank. An apostle is a rock-solid ancient landmark that God sets for His Church.

In other words, an apostle is a bonafide "big shot" in God.

I believe that God does have "big shots," but I have to tell you that in 50 years, I have only met a few of them. I have met scores of "little shots" that would like to think they were "big shots," but they were always lacking in real spiritual authority. They may have had a title and a degree, along with a position and a big brown desk, but real authority is earned, not granted.

Authority in God only comes from years of brokenness. There is no easy path, and neither can you attain that position through scholasticism or education. Years of being a faithful Christian may gain you respect, but authority only comes through a deep fear of the Lord. Even Jesus feared God, the Bible says, and it not only made Him of quick understanding (Isa. 11:3) but also gave Him his authority in that He was heard of God (Heb. 5:7).

There is something about a man or woman who has the kind of authority in God that you can feel as soon as they enter a room. You don't even have to know who they are. You can feel it. It isn't their power that you feel; it is the power of the anointing of God that is upon them. When you are in the presence of such a person, somehow, deep in your soul, you know it is time to shut up and pay attention.

So, what of all these self-appointed apostles we have running around all over the place? Some of them have huge followings and big churches, while others are more like "apostles-at-large" running around proclaiming their vaunted positions so that we will all know who they are.

I just have to laugh. They look like children to me, playing at being religious. Some of them are so lightweight that you feel like the next breeze could come along and blow them away.

"Oh, but they are such nice guys!" Nice guys, don't cut it. Which of the apostles and prophets in the Bible were nice guys?

"But they have done so many wonderful things!" Yeah, so did Mahatma Gandhi, and where did he end up?

All this would not be a big deal if it wasn't that these deluded apostles had taken it upon themselves to lead the Church. They do not possess the power to stand against the powers of darkness and, as a result, will lead those who follow them into a weakened state of faith and will set them up for a fall.

You see, the fear of God not only gives you authority and power, but it also gives you spiritual wisdom and understanding. Without it, your depth in God can only go skin deep. And that is exactly what Satan wants -- a weakened fear of God that is more akin to "respect" or "reverence" than to the strong "fear and trembling" that the Word of God dictates (Ps. 2:11, Eph 6:5, Phil. 2:12). A church without the strong leadership that only a true apostle who really fears God can give, is like a city without walls – defenseless and naïve, never aware of the danger lurking over the horizon. A dangerous place to be, but one that is all too common in our modern church world today.

Paul said that perilous times would come (2 Tim. 3:1), and that peril would come from within the church. And so it has.

> *"Having a form of godliness, but denying the power thereof: from such turn away. For of this sort are they which creep into houses, and lead captive silly women laden with sins, led away with divers lusts, ever learning, and never able to come to the knowledge of the truth."* 2 Timothy 3:5-7

Serving the Lord in the Prayer Room

I am always excited when I hear from the Lord. What great confidence it gives you when the Lord pierces through the fog of the world around you and touches your heart!

That doesn't mean that every message from the Lord is about something good. Often, it is a word of reproof to sharpen your vision to see through the dark shadows that can creep into the path before you. Nobody likes to get stripped down, but afterward, it will yield the peaceable fruit of righteousness and set you back on a solid pathway so you can see clearly again.

This morning, the Lord reminded me of a message that I have brought to others. (He does that a lot.) Whenever you preach a message under the anointing of the Holy Spirit, you have little control over what comes out of your mouth – it's as if you are tossed into a river that is running downstream, and you are just along for the ride. What you say during those times not only applies to others, but it also applies to yourself.

These past few months, the Lord has been stripping me down to bare metal. He has taken away all the props that have held up my ministry, from the radio broadcasts, ministry to others, and even to my trips overseas to evangelize. It's like I got stuck on a shelf.

Now, He did not do this without warning. I knew beforehand that He was about to drag me into a solitary place deep into a desert. I just didn't know how far. It was so far that I was beginning to wonder if I would ever come out of it. Everything was stripped away until I felt like I had nothing left of any ministry I might have had at one time. I was left with nothing but a seat in a quiet, solitary desert.

As the noise around me began to subside into a deep silence, I found myself wringing my hands, crying out for something to do to serve the Lord -- but there was nothing. I began to feel abandoned, wondering what I had done wrong.

And then He reminded me of a message that I have preached several times to others.

Serving the Lord is not measured by what you do on the streets, behind the pulpit, or in the church. The real essence of serving the Lord is not measured by what you do but by how much you surrender to Him and let Him do. It all happens in the prayer room.

The only place that battles are fought and won is in the prayer room. You can't win a victory in the streets unless you have first won it in prayer. Only when you go forth with the knowledge that you have contended in prayer all the way up to the Throne of God and have won your hard-fought battles, can you ever go forth in confidence to fight the battles outside. Without that victory, you will not have the power, the anointing, or the effectiveness of the Holy Ghost to do anything for God.

Serving the Lord is done in the prayer room!

I can hear the echoes of my messages preaching back at me. I guess everything had to be stripped away so that it would be quiet enough to hear my own voice reprove me.

The Problem with the Sinner's Prayer

Well, I got another complaint this week about the Sinner's Prayer on my website. I get them all the time.

You know, I have never been able to figure out what it is about the Sinner's Prayer that gets some people so riled up. If they all had the same reason, at least it might make some sense, but everyone has a different reason.

One person will ask me where the Sinner's Prayer is in the Bible (as if it is part of some theatrical script), and another will tell me that I am giving false hope to people by making people think they can get saved with a prayer. (I thought that was the point.) Next, someone will chide me that it is supposed to be a personal thing, or complain about it being too broad, or that it is man-made and a product of the 20th-century revivalists, etc., etc.

Scheesh! What's a guy supposed to do?

Now, I could understand if the complaints were coming from sinners, but they never do. It seems that sinners understand what the Sinner's Prayer is all about; they just don't want to do it. No, the complaints always come from people claiming to be Christians who, most of the time, are gracious enough to warn me that I am going to Hell because of my stand on this prayer.

Nice folks. Reminds you of a bunch of siblings who can't get along with each other.

So, what is the big deal about the Sinner's Prayer? And why am I going to Hell because I believe in a sinner's prayer? And who asked them anyway?

Perhaps it just makes them feel righteous to stand on a soapbox and warn me of the error of my ways. I wish they'd take that zeal out to the streets and witness to lost souls. Then again, maybe that's not such a good idea.

What gets me is that I have seen with my own eyes the incredible power of the Spirit of God fall upon literally thousands who have asked Jesus Christ to forgive them and save their souls through a simple sinner's prayer. I have seen the instant, miraculous transformation as the Spirit of God would sweep over them and that climatic look of victory in their eyes as they felt the power of the Blood of Jesus lift their sins and set them free. What a feeling to be free, finally free, from the chains of sin and darkness!

I've seen this so many times that it wouldn't matter where I had gotten the Sinners Prayer from –

it just plain, flat-out works! Now, how can you argue with the power of God?

But then, maybe that's the point – it really does work, and Satan hates that prayer more than anything in this world, so he stirs up a fuss and throws out any reason he can come up with to attack it.

But you know what? Jesus Christ gave His life so that a repentant sinner like me could have the opportunity to say that prayer and dump a load of sin at the foot of the Cross and ask Jesus Christ to be my personal Savior.

It still works today, just like it always has. All you have to do is ask, and God will hear your cry for salvation.

Now, what's the problem with that?

"… and with the mouth, confession is made unto salvation." Romans 10:10

Marriage

Marriage is a big deal with God. It is much more than an act of convenience of co-habitation, procreation, or a tax break from the IRS. From the very beginning, marriage was ordained as a picture of our relationship with God.

From the courtship to the kids, every aspect of marriage is related to that covenant relationship with God. When we look at it in that way, the seriousness of the covenant that we enter when we say, "I do," becomes clear.

The Lord went to great lengths to woo us as His Bride. He paid for us with His own Blood, and the dowry that we bring to Him is our lives, dedicated to being joined as one flesh to His Body. We are no longer our own, but we enter into a relationship that is now pointed to God. It is an inescapable covenant that can only be broken by spiritual adultery with sin.

As we stand at the altar and pledge our lives to one another, we form a union with the Lord. A change happens to us that is mystical beyond what we can see with our eyes. We will never be the same again. We are now married, and even our name has been changed.

But marriage, like salvation, is only a threshold to a continued walk in our covenant relationship. From that point forward, we must also continue in our relationship to keep it strong. As we bond together, we find a synergy in that relationship that makes us more than what our individual lives could have amounted to.

And so it is in our walk with God. We have to make an effort to grow together in order to stay together. Christians that get saved but fail to seek the face of the Lord will find themselves with little more than a Baptismal Certificate to point to as evidence of their marriage to Christ. They may end up with a form of godliness, but they deny the power thereof as a result (2 Tim. 3:5). Small consolation in the Day of Judgment.

Satan hates a godly marriage as much as he hates salvation, and he will work hard to destroy them both. Just as he will work to tempt a Christian to sin, so will he tempt a spouse to lust. If he cannot succeed in the temptation to be unfaithful, he will try to steal our victory through accusations against ourselves and each other.

It is written that where two or more are gathered, there God will be also. Satan knows that as soon as you open up to another believer, his deception will be broken, so he will whisper to you to not tell your spouse, leaving you with a feeling of guilt and separation from the one you should be most connected to.

Failing there, Satan has one last tactic that he finds most damaging. He will do everything he can to convince your spouse of the accusation that he failed to convince you of and will try to block their ability to see through the spiritual attack you are facing, thereby driving a wedge into your holy covenant. If he can do that, he has defeated both of you in one demonic thrust.

But when we come to Jesus with our trials and struggles, He is there for us to turn the battle against sin, and to join together with us in a unified marriage that Satan cannot break.

That is why Satan hates marriage so much.

And a threefold cord is not quickly broken.
Ecclesiastes 4:12

Heart vs. Head

I've always been somewhat put off by theological scholasticism. Not only does it not fit with anything in the Bible, but it tends to make idiots out of reasonably intelligent men.

Oh yes, I've heard the worn-out retort to "Study to show thyself a workman approved," but study what? I always thought that meant study the Bible. After all, the Scriptures tell us that it is the Bible that is profitable for doctrine, reproof, correction, and instruction, so that the man of God may be "perfect, thoroughly furnished unto all good works" (2 Tim. 3:17). In other words, what else do you need?

This argument has been going on since the Garden of Eden, when Eve got suckered into thinking that the fruit of the Tree of Knowledge would make her wise. Sorry, Eve. It only brought death. And that wasn't all that smart.

We are always looking for a way to become "wise," as if we want something better than what's written down in that dusty old Book. So, we gobble up tons of Christian self-help books, videos, and commentaries in a never-ending pursuit to make us better Christians. But has it worked?

The part of you that hungers and searches for Truth is not your mind – it is your heart.

Solomon tried figuring out Truth but came to the conclusion that the effort was all vanity and vexation of spirit. He said the Fear of the Lord was true wisdom. Forget all the other stuff.

Which of the Apostles, prophets, or other great men of God based their power in God on how much stuff they knew? Even Paul counted all his intense theological training as nothing but "dung."

No, the Kingdom of God is not in word but in power, and you don't get that from a book. (Sigh) But we do keep trying, don't we?

The carnal mind is blind to spiritual things. Only with the heart can we see God, and with the heart, man believeth unto righteousness (Rom. 10:10). That's why it is so frustrating to argue with intelligent people who believe in evolution, abortion, gay rights, and many of the other popular social and scientific issues of today's humanistic society. If you fight the battle with their weapons, you will never win their hearts.

I learned something early in my Christian life about the simplicity of the Gospel that has always proven itself true: preach the Blood of Jesus Christ and the simplicity of the Cross. That's what will resonate with that tiny mustard seed of faith in people's hearts, and they will believe unto Salvation.

And the rest … well, unfortunately, I guess they will find out the Truth soon enough.

> *"And he said unto him, If they hear not Moses and the prophets, neither will they be persuaded, though one rose from the dead." Luke 16:31*

Be Still

There is a depth to silence that the carnal mind is not able to comprehend.

We often feel more secure when a cloud of noise surrounds us in our daily lives as if it was a buffer to cover us from issues of life that we either do not understand or would rather not face.

But there are times when we are faced with a heavy spiritual silence. When we are, we scramble for that reassuring feeling, like gravel beneath our feet, of the daily issues in life that we know how to deal with. It is times like these that we are forced to reflect on the stark reality of Eternity and our tiny place in the eternal scheme of God.

Prayer times are like a good weathervane. It is great when my prayer times are filled up with all sorts of things, and I can jump off from one thing to the next and feel like I'm actually getting right up to the Throne of God and accomplishing something. That's a good feeling – that God not only can hear you but that He is also paying attention to what you are praying about. You walk out of the prayer room with a sense of accomplishment, and you are ready to face the day with a confidence that you have won in prayer.

But sometimes it isn't like that.

Have you ever had prayer hours when you feel like you have been dumbed down and can only sit there mumbling about something mindless? There may be a million issues to pray about, but you can't think of any at the moment, and you just can't seem to get off the ground. You repeat your prayers like a monotone tape recorder, but it doesn't come from your heart. So, you stand up and walk back and forth to get some juice going in your prayers, but you feel like a tin soldier marching back and forth.

You know God can hear, but is He listening?

Where are all the fireworks? What happened to that vibrant flow of excitement that comes when you can feel yourself reaching Heaven? Did I do something wrong, or am I running down a wrong direction? Or is God just tired of me, and is paying attention to someone else right now?

And the answer comes back in a reassuring, quiet voice,

"Be still, and know that I am God." *Psalms 46:10*

Foundations of Freedom

Much has been debated in the last generation of the true roots of America. In the name of political and social expediency, we have slowly moved away from the rock that America's true foundations were set upon.

However, I would like to point out a few reminders of what our freedom was really based on.

Did you know that 52 of the 55 signers of The Declaration of Independence were orthodox, deeply committed Christians? The other three also believed in the God of scripture, His personal intervention in the affairs of men, and the Bible as the divine truth. There are so many stands that our original Founders made for the institution and inclusion of true Christianity into our unique government that they cannot be included in a mere one-page article, and yet they have been all but forgotten, erased, or, at best, twisted from their original settings so that we no longer understand what gave those incredible men the vision to establish a government that has never seen its equal in all recorded history.

I like what Patrick Henry said the best. Patrick Henry, who is called the firebrand of the American Revolution, is still remembered for his words, "*Give me liberty or give me death,"* but in our current textbooks, the context of these words is deleted.

Here is what he really said:

"An appeal to arms and the God of hosts is all that is left us. But we shall not fight our battle alone. There is a just God that presides over the destinies of nations. The battle sir, is not of the strong alone. Is life so dear or peace so sweet as to be purchased at the price of chains and slavery? Forbid it almighty God. I know not what course others may take, but as for me, give me liberty, or give me death."

Was Patrick Henry a Christian? The following year, 1776, he wrote this:

"It cannot be emphasized too strongly or too often that this great nation was founded not by religionists, but by Christians; not on religion, but on the Gospel of Jesus Christ. For that reason alone, people of other faiths have been afforded freedom of worship here."

How true. Freedom is not based on political savvy, modern technological advances in warfare, or even the democratic process. It is a gift from God so that others may find an open path to true freedom for the human spirit, which only comes through salvation in Jesus Christ.

But we have forgotten that and have scorned those old-fashioned ideas to replace them with a more modern view of life, thinking that we are more sophisticated now and therefore wiser. We have developed a new way of looking at life, ... and so the downhill slide began.

Although it is clear from history that the Bible and the Christian faith were foundational in our educational and judicial system, there was a radical change of direction in the Supreme Court in 1947 when they banned a prayer that declared our dependence upon God.

Then in 1963, the Supreme Court ruled that Bible reading was outlawed as unconstitutional in the public school system. The court offered this justification:

> *"If portions of the New Testament were read without explanation, they could and have been psychologically harmful to children."*

Bible reading was now unconstitutional, even though the Bible was quoted repeatedly by those who wrote our constitution and shaped our Nation and its system of education, justice, and government. In 1965, the Courts denied as unconstitutional the right of a student in the public school cafeteria to bow his head and pray audibly for his food.

In 1980, Stone vs. Graham outlawed the Ten Commandments in our public schools. The Supreme Court said:

"If the posted copies of the Ten Commandments were to have any effect at all, it would be to induce school children to read them. And if they read them, meditated upon them, and perhaps venerated and observed them, this is not a permissible objective."

Is it now not a permissible objective to allow our children to follow the moral principles of the Ten Commandments? And yet, James Madison, the primary author of the Constitution of the United States, said this:

"We have staked the whole future of our new nation, not upon the power of government; far from it. We have staked the future of all our political constitutions upon the capacity of each of ourselves to govern ourselves according to the moral principles of the Ten Commandments."

How far we have fallen in a mere 245 years!

Knowing the true foundation of our American freedoms, I hear the echo of Patrick Henry's famous call in the firm stand made by Joshua in his final plea to his people:

> *"And if it seem evil unto you to serve the LORD, choose you this day whom ye will serve; whether the gods which your fathers served that were on the other side of the flood, or the gods of the Amorites, in whose land ye dwell: but as for me and my house, we will serve the LORD." Joshua 24:15*

A more ominous warning calls to us from the ancient wisdom of Solomon:

> *"Be not wise in thine own eyes: fear the LORD, and depart from evil ..." (Prov. 3:1-7)*

May God Bless America.

Whoredom and Wine

> *"Whoredom and wine and new wine take away the heart." Hosea 4:11*

Hosea gives one of the most severe indictments of the church world in the last days, but it is hidden by the setting of the times in which it was written. Nevertheless, clues are scattered throughout this prophetic book that point to the times we are living in.

I have often wondered why God obscures His messages the way He does. You would think that He would make everything obvious so that we would all know what He is talking about, but that has never been the case.

It is more than just "the glory of God is to conceal a thing" so that we will make an effort to search it out. Righteousness in God is not a puzzle or a brainteaser, and we do not get points for being clever. If that was the case, then the line for salvation would be drawn at a certain IQ point, and those of us who didn't score that high would have to burn in Hell.

But that would be like making a bunch of tin soldiers and throwing away the ones you didn't do a good job on. Whose fault would that be? Do we have to burn in Hell just because God didn't do a good enough job on us? No, there is something more to it than just bad craftsmanship on God's part, or else the judgment of God would not be righteous.

And yet, even Jesus spoke in parables so that those who had ears could hear, and those who did not ... well, let's just say they should have been listening.

Isaiah chapter 6, in which the Lord says He will stop up the people's ears so that they cannot hear and therefore repent, is a passage that is referred to repeatedly in the New Testament: "He that has ears to hear, let him hear" (Matt. 11:15).

At one point in Thessalonians, it is even written that God would send strong delusion so that people who did not have a love of the truth would believe a lie. (2 Thess. 2:10-12)

I gotta tell ya, this is pretty scary!

We all read the same Book, so how is it we come up with so many different versions of Truth? Is it simply a matter of "different strokes for different folks"? If that is the case, then would anything matter? Anything goes!

Or is it just the "luck of the draw"? Some of us figure it out, and some of us don't? That's more like playing the lottery with your eternal soul -- and I reckon the odds for winning would be about the same.

Worse, we tie up our personal religious beliefs with a ribbon and decide the version we would prefer to believe in, and then hang onto it with a death grip. Did you ever notice how hard it is to convince someone that their religious beliefs are wrong, no matter how far off the Scriptures they may be? Please don't get me confused with the facts!

As I was praying about this last night, I prayed for God to raise up mighty men and women with power – real power – in God so that people would hear and see the Truth, but then the Lord reminded me that even that wouldn't work. People may be amazed at the miracles, but as soon as you say something that contradicts one of their tightly held beliefs, they will reject you. It happens all the time.

Jesus said that even if someone came back from the dead to tell them, they would not repent.

Truth is forged in hearts that, in all humility, seek only after the righteousness that flows with the Spirit of the Lord. The Spirit and the Word agree (1 John 5:7-8). You will only find that in a place where there is a manifest presence of the Holy Ghost and not in some reliance upon the traditional tenets of religion.

Donning religious clothing does not change your heart. Adhering to religious axioms of your choice only justifies spiritual pride. And going through the motions only makes you deaf.

This is the religious world that Hosea addressed, crying that a spirit of whoredom had entered the church, causing them to deafen their ears and fall into a religious sin. Their hearts were taken away, and they could not repent.

The race is not to the swift, neither to men of great means nor intelligence, but it is to those who believe the foolishness of the gospel. It is with them that God is pleased – those who are willing to humble themselves to seek the beauty of holiness in the fear of God, regardless of the religious baggage they have to throw away.

Those are the ones who have ears to hear.

Devouring That Which is Holy

> *"It is a snare to the man who devoureth that which is holy, and after vows to make enquiry." Proverbs 20:25*

I'm bothered by something I saw on TV the other day.

Throughout the course of an interview, the President of a large denomination spoke about having a "sweet spirit." This is how he wanted to portray his denomination and what he thought was how all Christians should be – just like "sweet Jesus." As President, he had decided that he only wanted to work with those who had that same "sweet spirit" and reject all those who were "grumpy" and who were "so angry over the pulpit."

"You know who they are," he commented.

You mean like the guys I read about in the Bible?

How in the world did this wimp get elected to lead one of the strongest denominations in America? Is it because he represents the new, "kinder, gentler" gospel that modern Christianity has been leaning toward for the last 40 years?

Well, I suppose we have finally arrived there. A quick tour of our church services will verify that we all want to be nice Christians and never offend anyone at all. We just want to be "sweet."

Isn't that cute.

Well, I guess I'm one of those grumpy guys. I'm not nice and am not interested in trying to be nice. I want the Truth – black and white – period.

This anemic gospel has not strengthened the Church but rather weakened it by giving into the enemy's persuasion that sin isn't so bad, and God will always forgive you anyway, so why sweat it? We can just float around and "love on everybody."

Yeah, that'll work, won't it? Sinners will just come by the droves because you're going to "love on them." right? I suppose that by using that reasoning, Osama Bin Laden would have gotten saved if only he would have allowed us to "love on him." (Believe it or not, I have actually heard that.)

Sorry, but the Bible says that it is by the fear of the Lord that men depart from evil (Prov. 16:16). This "being nice" stuff would be fine if there was no such thing as sin, Hell, and the Devil. Unfortunately, we are at war.

If they are correct, then I have the same question that Gideon had – where are all the supernatural manifestations of the power of God in our churches? What happened? Is God on vacation?

Or are we trudging farther and farther into a spiritual desert where there is no rain, no outpouring, no miracles, and no great moves of God? Take a look at the preponderance of the thousands upon thousands of desperate prayer requests emailed around the world, and maybe it will sink in that something is missing. If God is "our Daddy," then why, oh why, doesn't He show up with the healings and miracles like He poured out upon us in times past?

Isaiah says that the days would come when the vintage would fail – the "vintage" referring to the outpouring of the Spirit of God (Isa. 32:10). Not only has the vintage failed, but it is getting drier all the time.

O Lord, when will it turn around? And His answer is that we are not desperate enough for the Truth.

When we finally come to a place like Gideon's, where we realize that because we have left off to fear God, have pursued a gospel that is only interested in having a "sweet spirit" of blessings, peace and love, and have let the enemy dictate our religious mindset, maybe then we will come to the dead-end of realization that something is desperately wrong. Maybe then we will realize that we'd better take another look at the Scriptures and see what the personality of God is really like. He says He is a mighty man of war, not our "Daddy." He is a righteous Judge, not some wimp. He hates sin, not excuses it. He demands holiness and the fear of the Lord, not some "sweet spirit" and a weak, ineffective view of wickedness.

But it will be a while (probably a long while) before we get so starved that we are willing to turn around and return to the strong stand that our forefathers had established when they walked under the anointing and the power of the Holy Ghost. We're just not desperate enough yet.

Me? Well, just chalk me up as one of those "grumpy" guys who will not compromise with a weak, socially-correct gospel just so I can be "nice" and have people love on me.

A move of God is coming – it is written in Joel 2:23 – but it is coming to warriors like the ones in the Book of Joel who are on fire with the real, uncompromised, in-your-face, Heaven-sent, anointed-with-Power, hellfire and brimstone, repent-or-perish, not-worried-about-your-feelings Gospel.

We have devoured that which is holy without understanding the true nature of God and have based our religion on what we wanted it to be (and then made inquiries). The results have been predictable.

Only when we are ready for the Truth, will we see a return of an outpouring of the Spirit. Then we will see the prayer requests for healing get answered, and the pulpits thunder with the power of God, and the anointing begin to flow in our churches.

And then we will see the souls who are lost begin to make their way back to the altar.

Only then.

Mystery

"How that by revelation he made known unto me the mystery…" Ephesians 3:3

Everybody loves a good mystery, especially the ones that end up being so convoluted and complex that when the answer is finally revealed, it knocks your socks off. And the simpler the final answer, the better it is.

I love it when those stories get so complicated with unrelated clues that you can never figure out who did it. Every few minutes, you think it's a different person. And then, in the end, the hero puts the whole puzzle together in such clear, simple terms that you wonder why you didn't see it in the first place.

Did you know that the Gospel was a mystery? Although there were clues all the way back to the Creation, nobody could figure it out. God declared the end from the beginning, but He did it in such a way that we could never unravel its complex simplicity with our human minds.

Even Solomon, the wisest man who lived, said, "No man can find out the work that God maketh from the beginning to the end" (Eccl. 3:11). But hey, good luck trying!

The Jews prided themselves on their deep religious scholasticism, but the best they could come up with was a complicated system of rules layered upon layers of other rules that reached its pinnacle with the Pharisees – and we all know what Jesus thought of the Pharisees.

Prophesy is meant to be revealed, not figured out. God gets the glory, not us, so that when the prophesy finally comes to pass, you will stand back and exclaim that it had to be the Lord who did it and not man.

The Mystery of the Gospel reached its resolution on the Cross, but even then, God had to reveal it through the Apostle Paul's epistles before anyone could understand its fullness. Just to look back and see how God used the paths of the two covenants to merge into one final Truth, is just amazing. We look through the Old Testament and see the thousands of clues that were right before our face all the time – we just didn't see them. And that is the way it was supposed to be because "it is the glory of God to conceal a thing" (Prov. 25:2).

What a great story!

But there is more. The final mystery of God will culminate in the days that we are about to enter when the seven angels begin to sound. (Rev 10:7)

Who knows what God has in store for these days?

There is no end of endtime prophesy buffs who have written reams of endless theories. That is great for publishing another book for us to read, but when it is all said and done, I think God is going to do it His way, and that is rarely the way you would anticipate. He is the great mystery Detective (after all, He is the one who wrote the book), and we may find that, in spite of all our efforts to figure it out, the conclusion may still be the final mystery to be revealed.

> *"Let us hear the conclusion of the whole matter:*
> *Fear God and keep his commandments: for this is the whole duty of man."*
> *Ecclesiastes 12:13*

Foolishness of Faith

"Let Christ the King of Israel descend now from the cross, that we may see and believe."
Mark 15:32

How much easier it is to believe something when you see a sign! If we could just see a miracle or two, then it would be so much easier to have faith.

But God doesn't do it that way.

I noticed a few chapters earlier in Mark that immediately after Jesus fed 4,000 souls with the bread and fish, these same Pharisees came up to him and asked for a sign from heaven so they might believe.

What? Were you guys in the bathroom when all this happened? Or weren't you paying attention?

Contrasted against these religious skeptics is the Roman centurion standing below the Cross. All he saw was the death of Jesus, but that was all it took for him to believe.

Signs and wonders cannot change a person's heart – only the power of the Word of God can do that. Signs and wonders may show the presence of the Holy Spirit working in a man or woman of God, but it still must be lined up with the Word of God or it is the wrong spirit. (Satan can do wonders too.)

Faith is not based on what we see. It is based on the sufferings of the Cross.

There is something mystical about the Cross that cannot be analyzed and put into words, but it speaks to the hearts of those who hunger for the righteousness of God. You could prove the validity of the Gospel in a million ways, but it would never have the power to save one soul. But just mention that Jesus died on the Cross and shed His blood to save your soul, and those whose hearts hunger for God will hear you. It is the simple preaching of the Cross that wins souls. (1 Cor. 1:18,21)

There's just something about the Cross and the blood of Jesus Christ that transcends the realities of this life and speaks to a human soul. Those who have ears to hear will jump at the chance to follow Jesus Christ, even if it is to the Cross, while others will only believe what they want to believe no matter what you tell them.

And hence, we see two paths in Christianity: one leads to prosperity, blessings, and love because it sounds so good. Instead of the Almighty God who demands holiness, we have "our Daddy" who loves us and won't let anything bad happen to us. There is no price, no sacrifice, and no suffering associated with this path. It is such an easy path that even sin and worldliness lose their horrible specter.

The other path is fraught with suffering, pain, loss, and tears, and the price is higher than flesh wants to pay. Instead of leading up to grand feelings of self-esteem, this leads down to a humility on your knees, finding a place of repentance before God because sin appears as it really is – a rebellion so horrible that God created a just torment for eternity to pay for it, and so strong that only the Blood of Jesus Christ could overcome it. Thank God for his unspeakable gift.

> *"For after that in the wisdom of God the world by wisdom knew not God, it pleased God by the foolishness of preaching to save them that believe." I Corinthians 1:21*

A New Generation

> *"Because my people hath forgotten me, they have burned incense to vanity, and they have caused them to stumble in their ways from the ancient paths, to walk in paths, in a way not cast up; to make their land desolate, and a perpetual hissing; every one that passeth thereby shall be astonished, and wag his head." Jeremiah 18:15,16*

I have always believed that the Book of Jeremiah is a perfect reflection of the times we are living in right now. The same things that Jeremiah saw in his day can be seen today.

Back then, Jeremiah had to face a people who had come out of a superficial revival that had been held while Josiah was alive and tell them that unless they returned to God, destruction would surely come. They didn't believe him because it wasn't the message that they wanted to hear.

There was no cry for repentance or judgment. Everyone felt that since they were the people of God and had a show of religion, God must surely love them, so they flocked to the light and vain prophets that rose up and prophesied of prosperity and peace. That was the message that they wanted to hear, not this old-fashioned message of repentance, the fear of the Lord, and judgment to come.

Since so many of these false prophets were all saying the same thing, it was easy to believe that good times were coming and Jeremiah was just a cranky, old prophet who didn't believe in Love. Another old prophet put it succinctly, "Tell us smooth things. Prophesy unto us deceits" (Isa. 30:10). "... and my people love to have it so" (Jer. 5:31).

It was the same judgment that had been spoken to the Israelites of Gideon's time. They had allowed themselves to be taken in with a worldly worship and, as a result, had been taken over by their enemies. Their land that should have brought forth a harvest was taken from them, and they were left a persecuted and scattered people. The desolation was so great that Gideon had to thresh his wheat in secret.

Gideon's answer to the angel who visited him still echoes today.

> *If God is with us, then tell me where are all His miracles and deliverance? What happened to the power of God that our fathers have told us about? (Judges 6:13)*

The answer was simple – you didn't hearken to the prophets that God sent you who warned you not to mix with the vanities of this world. You thought this was a new, more sophisticated time and that you didn't need that old-fashioned message anymore, so you would only listen to those light prophets of peace and blessings, and you would not hearken to a message that you did not want to hear.

The same situation has repeated itself over and over throughout time, and we are seeing it again today…with the same results.

God will give us a certain space of time to repent, but we will refuse. Why should we repent? Our pastors and prophets have all told us that we are all so beautiful and filled with love that we don't have to. As it says in Revelations,

> *"…thou sayest, I am rich, and increased with goods, and have need of nothing; and knowest not that thou art wretched, and miserable, and poor, and blind, and naked" (Rev. 3:17).*

We have burnt incense to vanity and refused to walk in the old paths; therefore, God will raise up a new generation of believers who want much more than "church as usual" and who will be willing to fight for it.

There is something interesting about what Gideon was told to do. He had to sacrifice the 2nd bullock, not the 1st one. There is something about it that tells me that God will raise up a new generation, not the old established one, to bring about a new move of God. It will be new winebottles that will hold a new wine that the established religious order will not be able to handle.

The move of God will pass us by, and God will raise up stones in our place.

Going to Kenya

I have been to Kenya several times and have experienced one of the most vibrant times of my life. These people are so hungry for God that it is as if nothing else matters. The people we have ministered with do not have much in worldly goods -- as a matter of fact, most of the people I met had very little at all -- but they had a hunger for God that overwhelmed and dissolved everything else.

I've read parts of the speech that U2's Bono gave to the National Prayer Breakfast about the extreme poverty and need that is in third-world countries, and while that rings true, there is more hunger there than just for food. They are starving for more of God.

Since I was there last, their excitement has grown such that they have won hundreds of new souls, opened new churches, preached to thousands, and have seen scores of supernatural miracles and healings. And they believe that this is just the beginning!

I wish there was a way to accurately describe what it is like to be in such an atmosphere. I tried writing a book, the Kenya Diaries, but it hardly touched on what it was like. I took a few video clips, but although you can see the excitement, you can't actually feel it. I'd like to stuff it all in a bottle to bring back here, but there isn't a bottle big enough. You just have to experience it for yourself.

Even though there are many churches there, I found a lack of spiritual depth amongst their church leadership. There is a dearth of the old, time-tested spiritual elders to guide and lead the Church there. It was as if a whole generation was missing. Most of the pastors I found there had only been in the ministry for a handful of years, and it was from them that I heard of the desperate need for the greater depth in God that can only be found in those old warhorses of God. One pastor told me that they have no Moses' to lead them through the desperate spiritual warfare they face. That's pretty scary.

On this trip, Cindy and I will focus on the churches that are in Nairobi and attempt to share with them what we've learned in our Christian walk. We are not going to give medical help, build new buildings or dig wells – I don't have the money for that, and neither am I a doctor. What we are going there for, however, is much more valuable. We are going to teach them the basics of how to be a strong warrior for Jesus Christ, how to reach the Throne of God, and how to win souls. That's all I have to give anyone, but it is better than anything that money can buy.

Okay, so we're excited, but what about them? Are they excited? Well, let's put it this way – they have us scheduled morning, noon, and night for every day we will be there. They are planning on sucking out of us everything we know about God! Yeah, I'd say they're excited.

Picture this! Each day we will be at one of the churches in Nairobi. In the morning, they will gather together with us to read Bible, then after a short break, we will have a prayer meeting, after which we will head out to the streets to go witnessing. Then we will gather in the evening to have services, which usually last for 3 or 4 hours. It will be glorious! The schedule might kill us, but what a way to go!

The thing that makes this all so exciting, however, is not the schedule but the hunger that these people have. We are going to a people who are starving for God, and who never have enough – they always want more. They are like the people in Chapter 1 in the Book of Joel – they are so hungry that they will strip the vines bare of everything they can devour.

How many of you know that this has all the earmarks of the beginning of a great move of God? This is the way it always begins, and I am looking forward to seeing something so wonderful happen there that it will be spoken of for Eternity.

I can't wait.

God is Love

"He that hath the Son hath life; and he that hath not the Son of God hath not life." 1 John 5:12

What is this "life" that the Bible speaks about? What happens to you when you experience Salvation that so completely changes you that you can actually feel a transformation from death? There is something more here than spouting off a new philosophy about Life.

I hear a lot of people say they are a Christian because they believe in Jesus, but I don't see the evidence of a changed life in many of them. And yet, don't you dare tell them that they aren't saved or you risk being called judgmental. After all, aren't we are supposed to love everybody?

Is that true? It is so easy to spout off "God Loves You" – you hear it all the time – but what does that really mean?

We all know John 3:16 -- we may not know anything else in the Bible, but we all know John 3:16. What a comforting thing to know that God loves us, so we wave it around like a banner that encompasses whatever lifestyle we have chosen, knowing that in the end, we are going to Heaven because God loves us. But is that what John 3:16 really means?

There is a twist in that scripture that we often overlook. It does not say that we "would not perish" – it says that we "should not perish." We are given a choice, not a free ticket. The door is opened to give us an opportunity to enter into the kingdom of God, but it is up to us to walk through it.

I hear pastors tell us all the time that God loves the homosexual. Wait a minute! Is that what it says in the Bible, or are we simply repeating a time-worn expression that has been repeated so many times that we no longer question its validity?

People say that God loves the sinner but hates the sin, but the Bible says that God hates the workers of iniquity (Psalms 5:5). Which is it? God says He changes not, but we are constantly looking for a loophole.

What about Hell? Are we now excused because Jesus died? Jesus said that few there be that make it to Heaven, but are we now including in that few anyone and everyone who simply says they believe in Jesus?

Something is out of synch here with the Scriptures. No matter how many times we say otherwise, the overwhelming preponderance of

Scripture deals with judgment and righteousness, not love. Read it for yourself and see. If you want to be in the love of God, you must keep the commandments, for that is the Love of God (Jude 1:21, John 14:15, 15:10). That's what Jesus said, and I think He knows better than our conciliatory pastors.

God delights in mercy, but that mercy comes with the price of repentance. The grace of God is not cheap. God is, above all, a righteous God who will not excuse the guilty. If you do not repent, the wages of sin are still death.

When you spout off "God is Love" to everybody and anybody, what many of them hear is that they don't have to worry about judgment. The Bible doesn't say that. Are we trying so hard to escape the judgment of God that we are willing to cloak ourselves in a misguided rationalization so we can remain in sin? How is that love?

Does God still love the sinner? Yes, of course! It says He loved the world so much that He was willing to sacrifice His only begotten Son for us so that we might have life. But for those who reject that salvation and have chosen to work iniquity in their lives, the scriptures plainly declare that they have removed themselves from the Love of God and have placed themselves in His wrath.

The love of God is that Jesus died to set you free. You can choose to repent of your old sinful ways and accept Jesus Christ as your Savior and enter into the Love of God, but if you decide that you would rather hang on to your old sinful ways, then you have made a choice that removes you out of the Love of God.

Does God love homosexuals? Only if they repent.

> *I love them that love me; and those that seek me early shall find me. (Proverbs 8:17)*

Living Color

"Confess your faults one to another, and pray one for another, that ye may be healed. The effectual fervent prayer of a righteous man availeth much." James 5:16

We used to describe things as being in "living color," but today, kids want them in 64-bit color –another capitulation to the digital age. I prefer Living Color, but I'll take anything over the dullness of monochrome.

That's how I want my prayers to be – in color, alive and vibrant. Monochrome prayers just don't seem to get me excited, and they don't give me the feeling that I have gotten anywhere with God. Yeah, I suppose they work after a sort, but they sure are dull.

I want to pray like Elijah. Now that's a guy who knew how to pray!

Anybody who can lift his voice to the heavens and call down the fire of God ranks pretty high in my book for effectual prayer. And the fact that he didn't have to jump up and down, yell and scream, or go through all kinds of impressive gestures to get an answer emphasizes the point.

How about when he called upon God to stop up the heavens for 3½ years? Somehow, I don't think he got worried every time a cloud appeared on the horizon, wondering if it would rain anyway. "Oops, I didn't pray hard enough! I knew I should have stomped my feet a little bit more."

No, he just prayed. But he prayed in Living Color.

What was his secret? How was he able to have that kind of power in God? Was it that he simply had a mustard seed of faith – or maybe something bigger, like a coconut? Either way, how do we get that kind of faith so that when we pray, we get answers like that?

I believe that real prayer gets real answers, but real prayer does not come in monochrome. It takes more than barely making contact with the Prayer Department in Heaven to put vibrant color in your prayer life. All dull prayer gives you is some barely discernable shades of gray. Maybe it will work, and maybe it will not. (Sigh) Oh well, there's always tomorrow.

Jesus told us that we have to pray with a desperate determination that will drive us through the outer layers of prayer to pierce into the Throne Room of God. Consider the Unjust Judge (Luke 18:1-8). But that takes faith, lots of it, and that kind of faith must be built. You can't just turn on a switch and, presto, Instant Faith!

If you knew for sure that you would get a supernatural move of God if you prayed in living color with all zeal and fervor, but that you had to pray like that for hours and hours, would you do it? Could you do it? Easy to say, but would you have the faith to hang in there all the way to the end? That kind of faith doesn't come cheap, but that's what gets answers from God.

We know that the Word of God gives us the power to pray -- not just the reading of it, but it is the HEARING of the Word of God that gives us faith. You have to walk in the Spirit of the Lord to have ears to hear what the Spirit of God is saying in order for faith to be able to take root in your heart.

Okay, that makes sense. So how do we do that? Elijah did it, and it says he was subject to the same passions that we are, so if he did it, we can do it.

Well, there's a secret to Elijah's faith.

The Bible says that Elijah called upon the Lord "before whom I stand...." Elijah stood before the Lord all the time. He lived in that secret place of the Most High God, and it filled his prayers with Living Color.

The Landscape of Ministry

Picture yourself walking for miles with nothing but your belongings on your back and your family trudging along beside you. You finally come to a landfill with all its trash, broken garbage, and discarded building materials lying all around. Bits and scraps of plastic bags fly all around the area (for some reason, these pieces of plastic bags are everywhere no matter where you look). The smell of decay mixed with mud hangs in the air like a backdrop behind a stage that you are standing on.

This is home.

There's plenty of stuff to build a little shelter with. Why shucks, there are all kinds of rusted and bent scraps of corrugated tin, pieces of wood and broken lumber, and lots of cardboard for wallpaper to keep out the wind. And if you drape some old sheets over that discarded furniture you found and wedge a few rocks under it to hold it up, it will look pretty good.

Ahhh, home sweet home!

Now picture 20,000 people right behind you, eager to crowd in right next to your 20 x 20 spot, and you can get a picture of the kinds of places that I am visiting. Some of these places have little, if any, plumbing at all or electricity. Sewage and trash find their way to the dirt paths that serve as alleys in between the rows of tin shacks. A cloud of red dust hangs in the air wherever you go and gives the entire place an overcast of a dirty, dusty look. After a while, you get used to it and no longer notice it, but these people live in it, and it is all they know.

Christian evangelists don't come here. There are no visits from social organizations or welfare groups. The fanfare from televangelists visiting these slums is mute. These people have never seen any groups of eager teen-agers from some prosperous American church coming here to paint churches or build homes. No one comes here – no one, that is, but the three looming, dark, shadowy specters of Death, Disease, and Despair.

This is where I am ministering. Yesterday, I sat in a ramshackle stick home that looked like it came out of Uncle Tom's Cabin. A woman had walked miles to come to where we were ministering to ask us to come and cast out the demons that keep attacking her home, so we drove our little car over bombed-out dirt alleyways to this little 10 x 10 shack to pray over it.

As I look around, I realize that this is her home – she actually lives in this – and she is desperate for a man of God to come to help her defend it against some very real demonic attacks. Swarms of demon-possessed rats and lizards periodically run through this shack – over the walls, the ceilings, and the furniture. I tell her that people in America would never believe that – they would think she was hallucinating. She looks at me in disbelief. Why wouldn't they believe this? This kind of demonic presence is very, very real here in Africa. You don't have this in America?

No, we don't. We don't even know about it. Neither can we even begin to grasp the desolation that makes up the entire landscape here, nor the despair nor the sorrow. But it is like the air they breathe; it has become part of them.

I have no answers here. I can't get my arms around the enormity of the problem, and I can't see even the faint beginnings of the light of a solution. It is dark, dark, dark. I just know that I am here, and although I don't have much money and can't help their poverty, at least I have the Gospel of Jesus Christ to give them hope. No matter how bad it is here on this side of Eternity, there is the hope of peace and life for their soul, and an eternity with Jesus Christ.

He is the only one that truly understands their situation and the only one who can save them.

Manasseh

"Notwithstanding the Lord turned not from the fierceness of this great wrath, wherewith his anger was kindled against Judah, because of all the provocations that Manasseh had provoked him withal." 2Kings 23:26

I am always struck by the bedrock determination of the judgments of God. It is written that God is not a man that He should repent, but for some reason, that is a difficult concept for us to grasp because we have assimilated the idea that if we say we are sorry, all will be forgiven, and everything will be OK.

Well, maybe it will be forgiven, but that doesn't mean it will be OK. I've heard it said before that the judgments of God are like a great stone wheel, rolling slow but sure, crushing all wickedness under it. Simple apologies do little to stop great stone wheels. Once judgment is set, it is set.

But ingrained into our culture are two things that are unique to the modern age: the lack of a fear of absolute rulers and the lack of the fear of judgment.

We cannot grasp the fear that ancient peoples had for kings and emperors because democracy and the rise of the common people have eradicated their absolute power. We can read about the chilling fear and trembling that was upon the people who stood before these great monarchs, but our minds have no reference point to be able to grasp what that must have been like.

The lack of the fear of God's judgment is similar. As successive generations have watered down the Word of God, we get farther away from the stark lines of the fear of God that our forefathers once possessed. Either we are more enlightened than they were back then, or we are just plain stupid.

The judgment of God that was placed upon Judah because of Manasseh was proclaimed AFTER Manasseh repented before God and had come back to try and make things right with Him. His efforts gained him a reprieve, but it did not stop judgment.

So, shall it be with us. America was established on the Old-Fashioned Gospel that was based on the fear of God, but it has morphed into a theologically scholastic shadow of what it once was.

Where our services once thundered under the anointing and power of God, we now have animated social gatherings for Christians to listen to our pastor's dissertation of Scripture. We call it church.

Where we once looked upon God with fear and trembling, we now talk about "awesome respect for our Daddy" as we sit in His big, comfy lap.

Where we once emphasized righteousness, we now languish in a warm, fuzzy concept of Love.

And where we once believed that judgment, once set, was sure, we now have convinced ourselves that because God loves us so much, surely, He won't do all those terrible things to us.

But the great wheel continues to turn.

After 60 million abortions, the rise and predominance of homosexuality, the rampant saturation of lust, and the success of greed and corruption in our society, you have to ask yourself how it is that you really think God is just going to ignore everything and forget the mountains of sin that we have heaped upon ourselves. If the Lord were to halt judgment, would He not have to apologize to Sodom and Gomorrah? And if He did, could we really rely upon Him to be righteous?

I fear that He really is righteous and that He means exactly what He says, and therefore great judgment is determined upon us as a fallen nation and world.

And, to me, the proof of that coming judgment is in how few of us believe it.

Broken

"And he answered and said unto him, Master, all these have I observed from my youth. Then Jesus beholding him loved him, and said unto him, one thing thou lackest: go thy way, sell whatsoever thou hast, and give to the poor, and thou shalt have treasure in heaven: and come, take up the cross, and follow me. And he was sad at that saying and went away grieved: for he had great possessions. "

Mark 10:20-22

Woven throughout the Bible is a theme of brokenness. We see it in the Garden of Eden, through the Patriarchs and Kings, and all the way to the end. Mankind has continually attempted to reach a place in God through his own efforts, but it has been a struggle in futility. It is only through brokenness that we can ever attain that place in God.

It would be easy to say that it is simply a matter of acknowledging that we need God in our lives, but the idea of brokenness goes far beyond that. There is a layer to the human soul deeper than just acknowledgment of God's existence or even His sovereignty.

Joseph was broken in Pharaoh's prison; Jacob was broken on the way back to Bethel; Moses was broken in the desert; the prophets were broken before they ever heard from God; the disciples were broken with Jesus' death before they became apostles; Paul was broken on the road to Damascus, and Jesus was broken on the Cross. There is more than just an acknowledgment – there is a broken, crucified yielding of the very core of your soul that must take place before you can come to that secret place that God has prepared for you.

I have seen many who have worked hard in the ministry and have sacrificed everything only to reach a certain level and then stop. This place of relative success is a comforting place to be in, especially when you can enjoy seeing the fruits of their labors, but often the Lord requires more, and we don't want to give it.

We look at how hard we have labored, how much we have sacrificed, and how much we have done for others, and we can't see what else we can give. We are at a plateau in our Christian life that is high and of great accomplishment -- and we got there honestly! It's a good place to be, and we are content to abide right there and watch the fruit our labor has brought forth. But we no longer strive to be broken of our will, our ego, and our view of ourselves. That is when we become stagnant.

Brokenness has little to do with what we have done or sacrificed. It is a condition in the depths of our soul, not a state of mind. It is a place of complete and total surrender to whatever the will of God is for us, not caring, not complaining – just broken. Gone is our will; gone is our resistance; gone is our concept of self. We no longer belong to ourselves; we belong to God.

When our vessels have finally been emptied out of ourselves, they can then be filled with the glory of God. Even the vessels themselves must become invisible so that all someone sees when they look at us is the Light of Jesus Christ that is inside.

Just as we cannot receive anything from the Lord until our hearts are ready, so can we not receive the depths of the calling, the wisdom, and the power of God until we are broken.

Jesus was broken on that old Rugged Cross that the world might have life, and He calls us to follow Him.

Inspiration and Great Deeds

> *"As the hart panteth after the water brooks, so panteth my soul after thee, O God."*
> *Psalms 42:1*

Great deeds are done by men with great desires, and the heart of man is the furnace that forges those desires.

Knowledge won't drive you that far – it just makes you accountable. Wisdom may enlighten you and make you aware, but it is not the driving force of your heart. Obediently doing good deeds will make a fair show of going through the motions, but it is not inspired by the flame of passion.

We sit and listen to passionate preachers pointing us in the direction we should go, we read the books that are meant to get us moving down the right path, and we sing the songs that lift our souls, but those are only tools to help, not the actual driving force of inspiration itself.

As human beings, we need inspiration to lift us up over mediocrity. Something must drive us, or we will not be driven; something must draw us, or we will not be drawn. It is not in the heart of man to inspire himself to do great things in God; it must come from God. We know what to do – we just need the desire to do it.

I have preached a lot of messages and have had a lot of messages preached to me, but as the congregation files out the back door, I sometimes wonder how far the word that was just preached to them will go. We need more than that little bit of gas that the preacher put in our tanks to go much farther than the church door.

We can edify one another and hold each other up, but inspiration must come from the Throne of God. He is the only one that can light that fire in your heart with the spark that comes from the Holy Ghost. Now true, you have to bring fuel for the fire, and you have to continue to feed that fire, but the first spark comes from the Spirit of God.

It happens when you accept Jesus Christ as your personal Savior. A fire is lit in your heart that you never had before. You can actually feel the warmth! But it is up to you to keep the fire going.

All the preachers in the world, all the edifying stories from other Christians, and all the self-help books written cannot replace the wood for that fire. That wood comes from the Word of God and nothing else. There is no substitute. The Word of God was written in the Spirit, and that is what you need to pierce through the layers of flesh and mind to touch the innermost part of your heart.

Reading and prayer will draw you to God and will build a fire in your heart, but when you forget your reading and prayer, however, you forget your power in God, and eventually, the fire goes out.

God will put the desire in our hearts if we go up to Him and get it (Phil. 2:13); it doesn't just fall out of Heaven into our lap. And once we have it, we must continue to seek the face of the Lord to keep it.

So, life is a test:

Some people care, and some people don't.

Some will seek the face of God, and some won't.

Some will overcome everything in their way to serve the Lord, and some will choose the easy way out.

Some will cry out to God for the drive and desire to serve Him, and some will just wait for it to happen to them.

Some will depend on others to serve the Lord, and some will push their way through the crowd to touch the Throne of God for themselves.

Some will cause their lights to shine and their fires to blaze, while others allow their embers to grow cold.

Some will do great deeds in God, while others sit and watch.

Prima Donnas

"That he would grant you, according to the riches of his glory, to be strengthened with might by his Spirit in the inner man; that Christ may dwell in your hearts by faith; that ye, being rooted and grounded in love, may be able to comprehend with all saints what is the breadth, and length, and depth, and height;

And to know the love of Christ, which passeth knowledge, that ye might be filled with all the fulness of God."

Ephesians 3: 16-19

Lately, I've been approached by several Prima Donnas who think that they have been supernaturally called to be a great prophet, apostle, or some other kind of avatar from God. While they are almost always excited about what a great calling they have in God, I usually remain a little less than impressed.

From what I have seen over the years, true Christianity is not a matter of how great someone is, how great they think they are, how great their place in God is, or even how great God thinks they are. It is not about you, it has never been about you, and it will never be about you – true Christianity is about others.

When I read the above Scripture this morning, I thought about how the Apostle Paul must have also had his share of people who thought they were great in God. It's funny how these people are almost always young, intelligent, and zealous but lacking in any depth of the Word of God and unwilling to go through any serious subjection. They believe that they are going to charge off into battle to win great and mighty victories simply because they are special.

But Paul points out that, although the Spirit of the Lord will strengthen you and that faith will hold you, it is possessing the love of Christ that will bring you into the fullness of God. This is not the love of God for us but the love of Christ for others. Jesus Christ gave His life so that others could be saved.

He wrote in Corinthians 13 that if we possessed all the gifts and callings of God that exist, but do not possess charity, then all those great things count as nothing but a bunch of empty noise. If we do all the great and mighty works that can be done but do not have charity, then it was all done in vain. How easy that is to miss.

It doesn't matter how supernatural someone's calling is, how many great works they have done, or how much power they have in God. What matters is how much their heart yearns for those who are lost and what they are willing to endure to see them get saved. Everything else is just empty noise.

Jesus Christ was Charity incarnate. He was broken on the Cross, not exalted. He was yielded and crucified in total surrender to God.

But it was that surrender that won the greatest victory of all time because it was not for Him but for others.

Built On Sand

"And every one that heareth these sayings of mine, and doeth them not, shall be likened unto a foolish man, which built his house upon the sand: And the rain descended, and the floods came, and the winds blew, and beat upon that house; and it fell: and great was the fall of it. "

Mathew 7:22-27

I have some exciting news for everybody! I just heard that God will crash down on Arizona and pour out a fantastic revival there first before spreading it out to the rest of America. And guess what? Because He didn't come at the time appointed, He is going to pour out an extra portion on them. (He must've been busy and lost track of time.) At least, that's what some newly risen-up prophets are telling us.

But hey, wait a minute! Isn't that the same thing I just heard about Kansas City? And St. Louis? And let's not forget about all the prophesies about the revival starting first here in Dallas. (Be the first on your block to experience a revival in your town!)

Okay, guys. C'mon now. This is a joke, isn't it? Or is this like campaigning to get the Olympics to come to your city next year? Or like the circus is coming to town – everybody hoop and holler! Bring out the clowns!

Somebody has got to be pulling my leg.

No, unfortunately, these prophets are all serious, and that's what makes it so scary. Of course, they have thousands of followers because everybody wants to hear what they want to hear – they just don't want to pay the price to get it. How much easier to latch on to some self-proclaimed prophet that will appeal to your itching ears!

But the houses that they are building are all built upon sand.

They remind me of the prophets in Jeremiah's time that told the people that, because God loved them so much, He would drive the Babylonians away. But Jeremiah, the lone prophet who cried for repentance, was left standing in the rubble when it was all over.

What I have trouble understanding is why. Why is this much-touted outpouring coming first to your city? Tell me why you are so special. Why would God pour it out on you?

In the face of almost 60 million abortions, rampant tolerance of homosexuality, the expulsion of God from our schools and government, and the mediocrity of our churches, I find little to line up with the requirements that God has set in His Word to have a revival. The blueprint for revival can be clearly seen in the Book of Joel, but I don't see much evidence of it in our churches today.

We are enamored with ourselves, but the Word of God calls for broken hearts. We tout our blessings and prosperity, but God calls for repentance. We say that we are rich, and increased with goods, and have need of nothing, but God says we are wretched and miserable, poor and blind, and naked. We watch causally as the lost wander past our church doors with no intention of coming in because they are afraid that they will become like us, but we are not cut to the heart.

We honor God with our lips, but our hearts are far from Him, and the fear of God is taught in name only. (Isaiah 29:13)

But hey, it is so good to hear that we are going to experience a great revival anyway!

We are not building our house upon the Rock; we are building it upon the sands of our own mesmerizing wishful thinking. There is a price to pay for any move of God, but we are hoping to bypass that and win the Revival Lottery.

I hope you have better luck than the Jews did in Jeremiah's time.

Reproof

One of the most important things that you need to grow spiritually is to be able to receive reproof. But that is not as simple as it may seem.

Everyone appreciates being edified and lifted up, and we love to hear that we have done something well. Pats on the back and "attaboys" bolster our spirits, encourage us to keep going, and build our confidence to tackle even bigger challenges in our lives. Have you noticed that Pastors that deliver encouraging messages never lack an audience? We like them because they make us feel good about ourselves.

But the ability to receive reproof is far more important than listening to a "feel-good" message. We need encouragement, to be sure, but it is the reproof of the Word of God that keeps us right with God.

Reproof, however, is difficult to swallow and sometimes goes down hard. The reason it is so hard is that we all view life from our own personal perspectives. We have determined our own belief system over the years and measure everything we see according to that yardstick. Even when we know we are wrong, it is still difficult to relinquish those precious, closely held beliefs that have come to define us.

The Bible says that a wise man loves reproof, but a scorner despises one that reproves him (Prov. 15:12). If we stiffen ourselves to reproof, we are in danger of becoming a scorner – and a scorner cannot repent.

One of the things I tell young Christians is to first identify someone who you know is truly of the Lord -- someone who has shown a tangible manifestation of the Power of God, not someone that just sounds good or tells you what you want to hear. They may be very likable preachers, but I dare say none of the prophets or great men of God were very "likable." It might be "nice to be nice," but it doesn't strengthen your soul.

If I see the tangible power of God present in someone, then I just have to figure that God must think they're okay. If that power is not present, however, then it's just a crapshoot -- maybe he's good; maybe he's not. How are you supposed to know? Just make a good guess?

We can always say that he has to "line up with the Word of God," but how many times have you heard that line used to defend conflicting doctrines? Everybody says they line up with the Bible!

Look for the power. The Spirit and the Word always agree.

I want to see the irrefutable, outstanding, supernatural power of God. If the preacher doesn't have the power of God that you can feel, then he's just another religious philosopher with a bunch of manufactured doctrines. Maybe he's right, and maybe he's not. Who knows? And really, who cares? I want God, not some cheap imitation!

Once you find a real man of God, then listen, hearken, and go in the direction he tells you. If he's got the power, he's got God – and if he's got God, then I'm going to shut up and listen to him.

The crazy thing, however, is that I have seen many who, as soon as he says something that they don't want to hear, will write that man of God off as being wrong and will turn away from him. We tend to defend our perspectives tenaciously in order to protect our pride from becoming bruised. Is that crazy, or what?

That is exactly why pride is such a dangerous thing. It is also why God honors the humble.

The ability to humble yourself so that you can listen and receive the reproof of the Word of God is the mechanism God uses, not only to correct us, but also to test our hearts to see if we are willing to put God above our own selves. If you cannot admit you are wrong, then it is your pride, not God, who is the Lord of your life. And if you don't let God rule your life, you will never grow in God.

Reproof is not only hard to receive; it is also hard to give. One of the hardest things a pastor has to do is to throw "nice" out the window and tell the truth. But, if a preacher has to worry about hurting your feelings, then you have rendered him ineffectual and have cut yourself off from the very thing that can bring you to righteousness. It takes guts to preach the truth without regard for the sentimentalities of sin, but weak messages produce weak congregations. It takes a strong message to produce a strong congregation.

Crowds may flock to "feel good" ministries to insulate their egos from ever having to get rebuked, but when it is all over, and we stand before God, it will be those who were willing to surrender to the reproof of the Word of God who will make it in.

> *"... reprove, rebuke, exhort with all longsuffering and doctrine. For the time will come when they will not endure sound doctrine; but after their own lusts shall they heap to themselves teachers, having itching ears; And they shall turn away their ears from the truth, and shall be turned unto fables."* 2 Timothy 4:2-4

"...reproofs of instruction are the way of life."
Proverbs 6:23

Death

Ever wonder what death is?

I realize that this is not a topic you would breach in polite company. Nobody really likes to talk about it much because it is considered a bit morbid, but seeing that it is every bit as prevalent as birth, why not? It's not as if we are going to get around it if we ignore it. Still, it is considered a "dark" subject for most of us to avoid.

But why is it considered dark at all? You know, from the perspective of Heaven, maybe it should be considered as Light instead. Of course, that's assuming you're going to Heaven. But from what I hear, it sounds like everybody is going to Heaven. Just ask anyone. They'll tell you. It's always the <u>other</u> guy that is going to Hell, not them.

But the real puzzling thing for me is figuring out how death actually works. True, if your body stops working, it will not sustain life -- kind of like a car that has run out of gas --, but there is something mysterious about how your spirit is released from the desperate clutches of your body and just flies away. Nobody really understands how it works -- you just die.

I remember a guy making a case for the existence of the soul by pointing out that the cells in every part of your body die after a few years, but your soul doesn't. It continues on. His point was that life is more than the composite makeup of physical body parts. The only problem was that this guy was a Hindu, which is where I got off the train. I didn't want to hear about blue gods with six arms or coming back as a Brahmin bull walking the streets of New Delhi.

Still, it made a good case against the bio-chemical theories of modern atheism. To atheists, Life is just the well-oiled function of a carbon-based machine. Nothing more, nothing less. Now that's dark!

Somewhere there is a switch that releases your soul when it is turned off. You can take a perfectly good dead body, pump the lungs up and down, and massage the heart all you want, but it won't return to life again. When the "you" that is you is disconnected, you can't crawl back in and start jumping up and down again. Yeah, I know that Frankenstein did it, but that doesn't work in the real world. Unless it was the bolts sticking out of his head that made it work.

And while we're on the subject, how does a baby become a living soul? You can grow a bunch of cells in a Petri Dish, but that doesn't constitute a human life – that's just a fungus. A fetus isn't some wart growing in your womb – it has a life of its own that is not distinguished by the mere multiplication of cells.

There is something miraculous about the life of a soul that cannot be analyzed in a textbook, debated on a Senate floor, dissected in a laboratory, or recreated in a test tube. It is something that God creates that defies understanding. He gives it, and He takes it away. That's what makes Him God.

How foolish for us to ignore that. Rather we should embrace the fact that we are given this gift of Life to use for His purpose (since He's the one that gave it to us in the first place). We have it for a short time to see how we will use it, and then we cross over to face the results.

Only in death will we understand the miracle of the soul that is not part of this physical world.

It is given to us to prove the existence of Eternity.

> *"Or ever the silver cord be loosed, or the golden bowl be broken, or the pitcher be broken at the fountain, or the wheel broken at the cistern. Then shall the dust return to the earth as it was: and the spirit shall return unto God who gave it."* Ecclesiastes 12:7

Cornelius

> *"There was a certain man in Caesarea called Cornelius, a centurion of the band called Italian band..." Acts 10:1*

Thus, began the biggest little revival in the Bible.

Imagine that you are Peter. You've been hanging out at the home of a believer named Simon, who tans animal skins for a living. Lots of wonderful things have been happening while you've been there, but time is moving along, and although you're content to stay with Simon, you're itching to get going. The Gospel is new, and there are so many that need to hear this message, so there is an urgency in you to run to every city and spread the good news. But until the Lord tells you to go, you know you have to wait. And wait. And wait.

Peter was notably an impulsive man. I'm sure waiting was not on his list of favorite things to do, but Peter walked in the fear of God and had learned to put aside all of his own ways and surrender to the leading of the Holy Ghost. Had he rushed off in impatience to another place to minister, I'm sure he would have had some successes, but he would have missed the three messengers that called him to come to Caesarea.

And where do these men bring Peter? To a Roman soldier in a notorious Roman city. Now, up to this time, the Gospel was only preached to the Jews because the Gentiles were considered outside God's grace, so you can imagine Peter's trepidation. There was no great crowd of people in some big auditorium waiting for the #1 man of God on the planet to enlighten them with a great message. No bustling crowds were pressing around Cornelius' house, waiting for Peter to touch them with the healing power of God. No, it was just a small handful of people who had no idea what to expect. And to top it off, they weren't even Jews!

Peter is ushered in, told about Cornelius' vision, and promptly given the floor. "God said you had something to tell us," he is told.

If you are Peter, you are probably wondering what is going on right now. All the fuss about coming all this way for a handful of Gentiles? This is not exactly what you were expecting. Where are all the crowds? Where is all the hoopla and fanfare? And what am I doing in the middle of these Gentiles?

Peter did the only thing he knew how to do – go with the flow. Tell 'em the Truth, and let God do the rest. And He did.

It is written not to despise not the day of small things (Zech. 4.:10). This humble little meeting ushered in the dispensation of the Gentiles and set a new direction for the preaching of the Gospel that resulted in, not thousands, but untold millions of souls that would eventually get saved. No little meeting, indeed!

How amazing are the works of God when we let Him have control! And how ineffective are our best efforts when we get in the way. When we are unwilling to wait on the Lord's direction, we tie His hands and miss out on the wonderful miracles that He had planned.

God doesn't do things our way, and He doesn't always make sense to the carnal mind. That is precisely why only a broken, crucified spirit that has surrendered to the Will of God can be used to bring about great moves of the Holy Spirit. When we rush about in our zeal to try to instigate great things, we may do some good, but we only end up being loose cannons. And loose cannons never hit the target.

Others will ratchet themselves down to follow a didactic set of rules that they have been taught in Bible College, thinking that they are following an organized plan that will lead to success, but end up denying themselves miracles. They prepare their messages, they concoct 5-year plans, they institute fancy programs and build new facilities, but the results are often just dry.

Peter could have rushed off in his zeal to some new place, but he would have missed the three messengers. Or he could have decided that going to a handful of Romans just didn't make theological sense and have held some manufactured revival somewhere else. But he didn't. He held until the Lord said, Go, and he followed in the direction he was sent.

And that made all the difference.

The Gift

"A gift is as a precious stone in the eyes of him that hath it: whithersoever it turneth, it prospereth." Proverbs 17:8

My grandson knows exactly what he wants for Christmas. He's told me twice now, but I still have no idea what he's talking about. How'd I get so old so fast?

On the other hand, my kids have asked me what I want, and to be honest, I don't know that either. Is that another sign of growing old? Or have I just grown content and satiated over the years?

I really had to stop and ponder about that for a while. I've got all the toys I want (with the exception of maybe a Jaguar XK8), and I don't really need more tools, computers, or a wallet this year. I don't dream of new household appliances. That's like giving your wife a vacuum cleaner for Christmas.

So, what do I want for Christmas this year? Well, I've put together some things I'd like to get from God. Maybe if He is making a list and checking it twice, I'll be found on the Nice list.

At the top of the list, I'd like to have more power in God. Not so I can strut around like someone wearing new clothes, but so I can present the Gospel of Jesus Christ in such power that it will touch people in the depths of their hearts so they will accept Jesus Christ as their Savior. I want the power to persuade souls.

I'd also like the gift of peace on Earth. As I read the Bible, however, I can see that as we approach the last days, peace will be taken from the Earth on a sliding scale. Since the Bible can't be rewritten, at least I can hope for peace in people's souls. In the face of impending darkness, I would like to see more and more people accept the Prince of Peace. Maybe I can't stop wars and poverty, but I can pray for the peace in people's hearts that overcomes all tribulation.

While we're at it, Lord, give me the Gift of Healing, not just to alleviate suffering, but so that others can see that You are still God. I get lists upon lists of prayer requests sent to me for so many people that are sick and oppressed that I can't pray for them all individually. Sometimes, I have to settle for placing my hands on the computer screen and pray for the whole list as one corporate whole. I would like something better. Something that I can see with my eyes that is instant, complete, and miraculous, instead of these gradual, hope-it-was-from-God medical answers. Something that gives hope that God really does hear us, not here and there, or now and again, or one here and one there. I want to see the power of God manifest like we have seen in generations past. Like Gideon, I want to see what our forefathers have told us about.

And what about a real solution to the crime, sex, and perversion that our up-and-coming generation is facing everywhere they turn? They are facing a world of darkness like we never imagined, and we need something real to offer them to turn them away from the deception of lust and hatred and worldliness that threatens to sweep over them.

I guess I could sum it all up into one gift that is the mother of them all – Lord, send a revival!

Sufferings

> *"I John, who also am your brother, and companion in tribulation, and in the kingdom and patience of Jesus Christ, was in the isle that is called Patmos, for the word of God, and for the testimony of Jesus Christ…" Revelations 1:9*

There has always been something about the recurring theme of the sufferings of the Body of Christ that has eluded me. Although it is written throughout Scripture, it is not something that is sought after very much. It's almost like huge boulders in our path that we acknowledge are there but try our best to find a way around them.

What is it about this theme of suffering that weaves though the Scriptures, especially the New Testament, that is so elemental to the Christian experience? No one wants pain (at least those of us who are sane), so we are naturally drawn to a more peaceful picture of the Gospel. Peace, blessings, love, prosperity – these are good things, and the promise of them stands out in the Bible as the rewards to those who follow the Lord Jesus Christ.

But follow where? Jesus went to the Cross and commanded us to deny ourselves, pick up our cross, and follow Him. That's not exactly what I would consider a favorite vacation destination (let's bring the kids and take lots of pictures!), and yet it stands out as a strong beacon to those who would follow Christ.

In America, we do not suffer the level of persecution for the Gospel that we read about in the New Testament, and neither have we experienced the depths of suffering that our forefathers went through to establish the religious freedoms we enjoy. We have resistance, to be sure, but nothing like what we read about in times past.

There are places around the world today where real Christians endure unspeakable persecution and suffering. The stories that come to us from these places are hard to believe and impossible to get a real grasp on. None of us would willingly trade places with those in such desperate pain. We feel horrible for what they have to go through, even angst, and we wish their lives were as good as ours.

And yet, they often feel sorry for us because we do not know Christ through the depth of suffering and persecution. That's the part that always gets me.

Just recently, a pastor in China was pardoned from serving a long sentence of torture because he was winning too many souls in prison. He refused the offer for an early release and demanded his right to serve out the rest of his sentence so he could continue to minister.

I have spoken to men of God who have suffered terrible things like that, and their responses are almost always the same. They glorify God for the honor of suffering for His name's sake. How do you answer something like that?

When you read the introductions in each of the Epistles, you can feel the intense fervor and passion that the Apostles had for the Lord and His church. Passion and intensity come only through suffering.

Could it be that we in the West are missing something? In our prosperity and relative peace, is it too hard for us to perceive an aspect of the Grace of God that defies carnal understanding? I know there will be those who will answer me that we are supposed to live under the blessings of God. Others have told me that we do not have to suffer because Jesus suffered for us. I do not agree. There is something more to the path of the Cross than easy living.

Richard Wurmbrand, the author of "Tortured for Christ," once said that those who have not suffered such persecution can never understand the glories of the grace of God that these martyrs have experienced. Perhaps we should re-evaluate what our faith is based on and look at it from a different perspective. Maybe then we would understand with a new clarity the desperate war between Light and Darkness.

It might change our view of our own Christianity.

> *"For unto you it is given in the behalf of Christ, not only to believe on him, but also to suffer for his sake (Philippians 1:29)*
>
> *... that I may know him, and the power of his resurrection, and the fellowship of his sufferings, being made conformable unto his death;" (Philippians 3:10)*

YouTube

> *"And Gideon said unto him, Oh my Lord, if the LORD be with us, why then is all this befallen us? and where be all his miracles which our fathers told us of, saying, Did not the LORD bring us up from Egypt?" Judges 6:13*

YouTube has struck a chord in people to make their own personal splash in the tide of humanity, and they have provided a place where, in one small spot on the World Wide Web, you can say, "Here I am." It's almost as if it lends you a sense of significance, or, to butcher René Descartes, "I post; therefore I am."

I waded through all the crazy stuff, the dumb stuff, and the porn to find a section about God and Religion in the sheer volume of millions of personal videos. Oh yeah, it was there all right -- if there is one thing people like to talk about, it is religion -- but it wasn't what I expected.

I got saved at the tail-end of a generation that experienced the power of God in church and knew what the reality of the Holy Spirit felt like. We had seen the great revivals, the huge healing ministries, and the over-powering presence of the Holy Ghost in our church services. But this generation has not.

And the reflection of that loss was seen in stark clarity on YouTube.

I was shocked at the volume of disillusionment. Hundreds of young and old ranted about the ineffectualness of religion, even to the point of declaring it as one of the greatest evils thrust upon the human race. The few who gamely tried to defend the Gospel were so languid that they did more to reinforce this backlash against faith than to be a testimony for it.

I was not surprised at the candor of these angry, young rebels because I remember very well a young man who, as a stone-cold atheist, made it a point in his life to mock the very idea of God, Eternity, and the stupidity of Christianity. Like these young people of today, I had seen no sense in believing in something that I could not see, feel, or touch and had been utterly amazed at seemingly intelligent people who did. If God was so big, then why, I wondered, did He not just go ahead and show Himself? After all, He did want us to believe in Him, didn't He?

All I could see was a great disconnect between faith and reality, and I was determined not to fall for such obvious stupidity as believing in a God who wasn't there. Didn't Time Magazine declare that God was dead?

In the same way, these kids today are not interested in hearing about your beliefs, and they see no validity in a book that they feel was written by men, so they will not listen to an argument that uses the Bible to prove God's existence. They want real, tangible evidence, or they will not believe.

When they go to church, they come out the same as they went in – unchanged and certainly not convinced. They've listened to preachers stand in the pulpit with dry, prepared messages with five bulleted points, and wonder what would happen if a puff of wind blew all those disheveled notes off the podium. They've seen nice Christians smile at them and tell them nice things that will not offend anyone or sound "negative," but they are digging for bedrock truth, not surface fluff. They've watched a seemingly endless parade of prosperity ministers explain how God wants them to be rich, but they are not looking for money. They want the real thing … if it exists.

Growing up on the streets of New Jersey, I had never heard about Salvation – never even heard the words "born-again" -- but then something happened to change all that – I got saved. <u>But</u> (and this is a big "but") I got saved at a little church where the power of God was so thick that, when you walked in the door, you could feel it dripping off the walls. No matter who you were or what you thought you believed, you could feel the supernatural presence of God. Services were packed with every kind of person you could imagine – from drug dealers to businessmen; from atheists to priests; from whores to housewives – all hungry to experience the power of God. There was a tangible power there that you could feel, but in 50 years, I have yet to find another place like that … and, unfortunately, neither have they.

All I could think of as I listened to these young people bare their souls was how much we had failed them. Here in the South, we are buffered by a conservative society that still believes in God, but outside our little world is a growing surge of people who want more than just empty words. They don't want to hear what you believe – they want to see it for themselves, and they haven't seen it.

How can you blame them? You cannot write YouTube off as the casual musings of some disgruntled teen-agers – these kids have taken the time and made the effort to create videos to tell the world how they feel. You can hear their souls crying out. And we haven't answered them.

I see in YouTube a picture of our society that is swelling up before us that has largely gone unnoticed. A challenge is presented here that must be answered, or we will reap consequences in this new generation that are very dark. Satan has thrown down the gauntlet before us and laughs at our weak response. Only when we once again find courageous men and women of God who know how to stand in battle and preach under the anointing of the Holy Ghost without worrying about offending anyone, will we be able to answer this tsunami of unbelief.

YouTube is a good place to start. I guess it's time to go get a webcam.

> *"And my speech and my preaching was not with enticing words of man's wisdom, but in demonstration of the Spirit and of power: that your faith should not stand in the wisdom of men, but in the power of God." 1Corinthians 2:4,5*

Twelve Stones

> *"And those twelve stones, which they took out of Jordan, did Joshua pitch in Gilgal. And he spake unto the children of Israel, saying, When your children shall ask their fathers in time to come, saying, What mean these stones? Then ye shall let your children know, saying, Israel came over this Jordan on dry land … That all the people of the earth might know the hand of the LORD, that it is mighty: that ye might fear the LORD your God forever." Joshua 4:20-24*

So where are those 12 stones now? It is written earlier in the chapter, "they are there unto this day." If that is the case, they've got to be there somewhere. Realistically, they are probably scattered somewhere, washed away, or under the pavement of some parking lot, but still, they are there somewhere. Good luck finding them.

Time, conditions, and changes have a way of washing away memorials, no matter how foundational they are. What happens when we lose our own 12 stones that were placed as a memorial to the foundations of our own faith? We forget that's what happens, and we construct in the place of their faded memory things more akin to the capricious paths we have chosen.

All things are relative to the present. We judge from our current perspective and measure everything according to what is now in vogue. We would rather forge new paths, try new things, and stay modern. New is interesting; old is stuffy.

But God is not a creature of fashion; He is timeless. We change; He doesn't. We work tirelessly to come up with new ideas; God rests on the same old concepts that were there in the beginning. There is a constant elastic strain between God and us.

That is precisely why God valued the monument of those 12 stones at Jordan. And yes, I believe they are there unto this day, but they are lost to the overlay of time and progress.

And it didn't take long to forget them. Within a few generations, Gideon wanted to know what happened to the great moves of God that his forefathers had spoken of. They had been forgotten, and as a result, the enemy now possessed the land that had once belonged to the people of God. This same script would play out repeatedly all the way to the end of time.

I have been around long enough to remember the outpouring of the Spirit of God in church. I have seen the miracles, have experienced the power of the Holy Spirit, have seen the packed altar calls, and have felt the thundering power of anointed preachers come over the pulpit. But now, the memorial of those foundations is lost to time, and very few remember what it was like. The stones have been washed away, and this new generation does not remember what they were all about.

It is not about believing that God exists. Belief is not Faith, and neither is there any power in mere belief. The Israelites that crossed the Red Sea believed God existed, but it was their unbelief, not their disbelief, that dug their graves in Sinai.

The 12 stones are there, not so that people would believe in His existence, but so that the whole world would remember that the hand of God is mighty -- a power that you can feel – and that we would fear God and keep His commandments.

We have lost both of those concepts. We know about them, but we've lost the 12 stones, and we have forgotten the strong foundations of righteousness that we once held so dear. That which used to be good is now too hard and judgmental for today's modern church. We have a better approach, a more modern one. We're smarter than the old brush arbor revivalists were, and we disdain the hellfire and brimstone messages that forged the fires of revival that established the foundations of those same churches.

Isaiah 29 tells us that two things deaden the church: 1) we honor God with our lips, but our hearts are far from Him so that we have a form of godliness, but we deny the power (2Tim 3:5), and 2) the fear of the Lord is taught as merely a theological concept instead of inhabiting the hearts of men (1Cor 2). These are foundational stones that have been dismissed.

The stones we should have built the church upon have been washed away, and in their place, we have built upon sand.

Sundial

"Hereby know we that we dwell in him, and he in us, because he hath given us of his Spirit" 1John 5:13

Lately, I've been dealing with a lot of young people who do not believe in God and certainly do not believe that the Bible is the inspired, inerrant Word of God. The most pointed response I have heard was, "There is no way you can know for sure that God exists, so why believe in Him?"

He has a point.

If the presence of God were totally absent from this world, why would you engineer your entire life around such a concept as nebulous as Faith? What possible reason could you offer for why you believe in God despite the lack of evidence?

I used to feel the same way. Why do you believe? Is it simply because that's the way you were raised, and since your mother told you so, that settled it? Or are you so miserable in this life that you are merely grasping onto any shred of hope that maybe there's a better way? Or do you fear death so much that anything is better than facing total oblivion?

These kids want some real answers; otherwise, they will not believe. Can you blame them?

My shock at the responses I received from these young people was not at their reasoning but at the fact that they had never seen an example of the real power of the Spirit of God. They tell me that they have been to church, but they saw nothing there that convinced them. And what they have read about sounds more like emotional imagination than a physical reality.

Why is that?

The only place we can lay the blame is on ourselves and the church environment that we have created these last couple of generations. Church is not like what it used to be, and neither is our society.

But what if you could walk into a church service and feel the overwhelming presence of the Spirit of God as soon as you walked in the door? When is the last time you found a place like that? Well, at one time, that was the rule and not the exception, but we are hard-pressed to find a place like that anymore.

But what if? If you found a place like that, you would not be able to walk out the doors without acknowledging that you just experienced something so real that you will never be the same. You may still reject it because you prefer the pleasures of sin, but you would not be able to deny it.

This is what our society is missing today – the presence of the Spirit of God.

You want to know why multitudes of souls are not flocking to the altars to get saved like they had at one time? You want to know why there aren't piles of crutches and wheelchairs left abandoned outside the church door? Has it occurred to you that we are missing something that we once had?

Well, it has certainly occurred to them, and they are not buying our excuses. They are not interested in all the cute programs we have to offer, neither are they persuaded because we are such nice people. They want concrete evidence of raw Truth before they give up their sins. The Bible remains in their view as a dusty old philosophy book written by a bunch of old guys – nothing more.

I read a great analogy the other day. Picture a sundial. Remember those old timepieces? Suppose you had never seen one before, and you were looking at one for the first time. You might admire the aesthetic shape, the intricate scrollwork, and the well-ordered lines of construction, but it would be nothing more than a fine piece of sculpture to place in your yard for an ornament. No matter how well it was made, it would be nothing more than a piece of art.

But let the Sun come out, and the whole meaning of that sundial is unveiled, and its hidden purpose is revealed. What a transformation!

That's exactly what the Spirit of God does to the Bible … and to church for that matter. Without the Spirit of God, the Bible is, as the Apostle Paul described it, in the "letter." And the "letter" kills, but the Spirit of God gives it life (2 Cor. 3:6). Without the presence of the Holy Spirit, church is just a social gathering, but when God starts moving, He transforms it into a Holy Ghost Revival.

It is written that the days would come when the flowing of the Spirit of God would fail (Isa. 32:10) and that we would experience a famine for hearing the Word of God (Amos 8:11). There would come a great falling away in the last days (2 Thess. 2:3), and we would walk through a spiritual desert. Perhaps we are in those days.

But it is also written that there would come a great move of God, greater than ever before (Joel 2:23). I am looking forward to that day when there will be no more excuses that there is no proof of God's existence.

Let us pray with broken hearts that that day comes soon. Our children need something real to believe in.

> *Let the priests, the ministers of the LORD, weep between the porch and the altar, and let them say, Spare thy people, O LORD …wherefore should they say among the people, Where is their God? (Joel 2:17)*

Courage

> *"Be strong and of a good courage, fear not, nor be afraid of them: for the LORD thy God, he it is that doth go with thee; he will not fail thee, nor forsake thee." Deuteronomy 31:6*

There have been times in my life that I look back upon and wish I could just go back for just a moment and change – times when I lacked the personal conviction to stand up and be strong, times when I failed to do the right thing, times when I lost courage. I was a failure not only in my own eyes but also in those around me. How I wish I could go back and do it over again!

That is easy to say, but if I were placed in those situations again, would I really react differently? And if so, what was missing in me during the times that I failed? The answer is always the same – I lacked courage, and if I am to make the right choice the next time, I need to find that courage.

At first, it seems that courage is an attitude you develop: get ferocious, get mad, become bold, lose your fears, take on the challenge and "Damn the torpedoes!" But those are only thin veneers that you present to those around you. True courage is something that must emanate from the depths of your heart and soul and cannot be manufactured.

I noticed that all the real men of God in the Bible and throughout history possessed a holy boldness that gave them the courage to stand in times of adversity. It wasn't because they were nice guys that God honored them, but because when they faced adversity, they reached deep into their hearts and grabbed hold of something that emboldened them to stand no matter how impossible the odds were that they faced.

Courage does not come from personal strength and determination but from surrender. You have to have something that is greater than yourself that you are willing to give yourself for. There must be something that -- win, lose, or draw -- you are willing to fight for no matter what the outcome.

In order to have that kind of courage, you have to have a vision.

Proverbs 29:18 tells us that where there is no vision, the people perish. Without that vision, you have nothing to drive you. Contentment does not make us strong; neither does satisfaction give us impetus. There has to be something that drives us onward toward something greater. When we lose that conviction, our strength melts to putty, and our courage dissipates to the empty echoes of worn-out slogans and words without conviction.

But the kingdom of God is not in word, but in power (1Cor. 4:20).

It is not a matter of what we know, or what we like, or what we believe, but in what we are willing to surrender everything for. What do we possess that we are willing to give our lives for? Like the heroes in Hebrews 11, what drives us to sacrifice our contentment and complacency on the field of adversity in complete disregard for whether we win or lose? We need a vision that is greater than us because courage is forged out of the fires of a vision.

Godly courage is surrender – surrender to the will of God in sacrifice of our own welfare so that others can be partakers of the grace of God and thereby shoulder their own cross and follow Jesus Christ. Courage is Charity – the surrender of oneself, out of love, so that souls can be saved.

The greatest courage of all was found on Golgotha. It was on the Cross where the vision for Eternity was given to all mankind.

Let us pray that God restores that vision to our land so that our Christianity is not marked by a desire for blessings, but for a victory won by the courage forged in those who are willing to hold up the Blood-Stained Banner.

Different in Texas

> *"When I die, I may not go to Heaven. I don't know if they let cowboys in. If they don't, then send me home to Texas, 'cause Texas is as close as I been."*
>
> *(popular Country song)*

What is it about Texas, anyway? It ain't the weather, and it sure ain't the landscape, but Texans sure are proud to be from Texas.

Let's face it, there are only two places I know of where people are so proud of where they're from that they're bustin' out all over about it – New York City, and yep, Texas. (At least we got a flag here in Texas; all the New Yorkers have is their Yankees baseball caps and coffee mugs with "I love NY" on them.)

Let's face it, have you ever seen anyone yellin' or hollerin' about being from Kalamazoo, MI or Hackensack, NJ? Nope, me neither.

Ask anybody here and they'll tell you, there's just something different about Texas. The funny thing is, it's true. And no, I don't know what it is either, but whatever it is, it runs through the soil of this land and shows itself in an attitude and character that you just don't find anywhere else.

It's just different in Texas, that's all.

Yeah, the picture we have in our minds is that cowboys are a little wild and crazy, with maybe a touch of rattlesnake eggs and barbed wire, and they don't much care for the bridles that polite society would put on them, but there are a lot of guts in their character. Cowboys don't care much about what anybody thinks of them, but when you're down, there ain't nobody better to count on. Underneath all the wild and crazy stuff is a bedrock of something rare. Integrity runs deep here. Deals that are made here on a napkin or with a handshake are more ironclad than any contract that a battery of New York lawyers could ever make.

As the song goes, "My heroes have always been cowboys," and when I look in the Bible, the heroes that I see there were cowboys also.

While Saul may have been an admirable choice for king, he measured himself against everybody else. With David, on the other hand, it was always about God. He didn't conform to what was supposed to be polite or correct and didn't care what anybody thought. He had the guts to stand up for what he believed was right.

David was a cowboy. (Well, he tended sheep, but you get the idea.)

So were Elijah, Phineas, Gideon, and on down the line. Even Paul was a bit of a cowboy. These were guys that didn't go with the flow, didn't care if they were popular, and had the guts to stand for what they believed in. There was a little bit of Texas in all of these men that made them stand apart from the crowd. They were just different than the rest. They wouldn't have cared if they were accepted around town, in any polite society, or even in the churches. They were cowboys.

Now, I don't expect to see God with a cowboy hat and boots, yellin' "Yeehaw" while He lassos us up before Him, but I betcha there's a whole herd of cowboys in Heaven whoopin' and hollerin'.

Oh yeah, I reckon they let cowboys in up there. I'll betcha cowboys are God's favorite kind of people.

Sunshine and Dirt

Sunshine and dirt … with maybe a little bit of water thrown in. That's all! Everything comes from sunshine and dirt. And scientists are spending billions trying to figure out how He did it.

From grass to milk and ice cream; computers and rocket ships to wood and sand and sea; from steel to human flesh – it's all made from some simple basic things that come out of the ground. And if you really want to get amazed, those things can be broken down into even simpler elements.

Have you ever wondered what God was thinking when He created the giraffe? Was He just having fun? "Let's see, if I take this nucleotide and switch it with that one over there in the DNA, what will I get? Oops, a platypus!" There are a lot of crazy-looking animals out there, especially insects, that are far beyond what any of our feeble imaginations could dream up. I wonder what He has in store for us in the next world.

I think one of the greatest proofs of Creation is Music. Now how did God come up with that? It ranks right up there with Love and Color. What an imagination! How did God dream up even the very idea of those concepts? And please don't brush it away with convoluted referrals to the magic of evolution as if Music just popped out of a Pre-Cambrian cloud.

I've read some idiotic scientific dissertations that attempt to explain Love, how color works, and why music affects our souls, but they end up sounding more like desperate attempts to discount the existence of God at all costs. You see, if they can't disprove God's existence, then they must acknowledge sin ... and that means there is a Hell, and that means you can't get away with sin. Uh-oh.

So, they keep trying in their attempts to exalt Science over Faith.

God made everything so simple that it is astounding, including Life itself, but the Intelligencia of modern society looks down on the simplicity of Faith as if it were the uneducated realm of the uninitiated and naïve. In their concept of the progress of evolution, Christians are placed somewhere between the ape and the scientist. They disdain Faith, but it takes a lot more blind faith to accept their theories about the origin of the Universe than it does to recognize the supreme omnipotence of an Almighty God.

Still, they keep trying. In their pomposity, they think they can create life in a test tube -- just give 'em enough time, they say. (While you're at it, can you manufacture a Universe? Or how about the dirt to make it out of?)

The deeper physicists delve into reality, however, the spookier things become. The string theory says there are 11 dimensions (that's down from the 17 they thought there were), but of course, that doesn't synch up with their other conflicting theories. If you want to watch them get really tongue-tied, try asking them to explain how Entangled Particles work. The more we discover, it seems, the more it points to God.

Nevertheless, instead of acknowledging the Creator, they want us to trust their superior intellect and believe them instead, and we'll call it Science.

At least Faith makes sense.

> *"Let no man deceive himself. If any man among you seemeth to be wise in this world, let him become a fool, that he may be wise. For the wisdom of this world is foolishness with God. For it is written, He taketh the wise in their own craftiness.*
> *And again, The Lord knoweth the thoughts of the wise, that they are vain."* *1Corinthians 3:18-20*

Mulberry Trees

> *"Therefore, David inquired again of God; and God said unto him, Go not up after them; turn away from them, and come upon them over against the mulberry trees. And it shall be, when thou shalt hear a sound of going in the tops of the mulberry trees, that then thou shalt go out to battle: for God is gone forth before thee to smite the host of the Philistines." 1Chronicles 14:14-15*

After we have won some victories in our spiritual life, there is often a tendency to fall back on past successes as the guide for whatever subsequent battles we may face. It worked the last time, right? Why wouldn't it work the same way again?

But spiritual warfare is not a function of some mathematical program where, if you input the same procedures, you will get the same results. We face an enemy that is very much alive, cunning, and scheming. Satan plans out his strategies like a game of chess – several moves in advance. He knows each of our weaknesses and sets up his traps in advance, hoping that we will let down our guard and fall into them sooner or later.

When David had been anointed as king over all of Israel, the Philistines realized that they had a problem. This was the same David that had sought refuge among them while Saul was king, and they were well aware of what he was capable of. They knew they had to attack David as quickly as possible before he became too strong and established.

The same thing happens to us. Whenever the Lord brings you into a new level of spiritual responsibility, Satan is quick to realize the threat that you have become, and almost immediately, he will attack. Suddenly, everything seems to go horribly wrong: things break, the money dries up, you get sick, people leave you, and a whole litany of things go bad. You begin to feel like Job -- every time you turn around, someone is telling you that the Sabeans have run off with the camels or something worse has happened.

We know the attack is coming from the devil, so we run to the Lord to defend us against the spiritual battles we are facing. Whenever we lean upon God, Satan is defeated. David knew this, and as soon as he was anointed king, he enquired of the Lord before facing his first battle. It was an easy victory.

But the enemy came right back to attack again. The first battle served only as a setup to lure David into the next one.

Had David followed the same battle plan as his first victory, he would have fallen right into the Philistines' trap, but David knew that every step had to be ordered by the Lord, so he sought the Lord again.

This time, God's plan was exactly opposite from the last one. This time, God told David to sneak around the back of the Philistines and wait. He had to listen for a "going" in the tops of the mulberry trees before he attacked.

In the Hebrew, the word "going" means a type of marching of the feet. David had to wait to hear the feet of the invisible host of the Lord marching before him through the tops of the mulberry trees before he moved. By doing so, God was able to go before him to win the battle and break the enemy.

Had David not humbled himself to seek the counsel of God the second time, he would have been destroyed, but he knew that victory comes, not by power, nor by might, nor by how we think, but by the Spirit of the Lord (Zech. 4:6).

Just because the Lord has led us in a certain direction once, that does not mean that we no longer need to ask for His guidance, even when the situation is exactly the same. When we forget our utter reliance upon the Lord, we will ultimately fall into Satan's well-conceived trap.

Faith is when we realize how much we need God. Presumption is when we forget that and lean upon our own understanding instead.

It makes the difference between victory and defeat, and it made a king out of David.

Natural Righteousness

> *"Thou crownest the year with thy goodness; and thy paths drop fatness.*
> *They drop upon the pastures of the wilderness: and the little hills rejoice on every side.*
> *The pastures are clothed with flocks; the valleys also are covered over with corn;*
> *They shout for joy, they also sing."*
>
> *Psalm 65:11-13*

Imagine waking up in the morning without an alarm clock and a tightly wound schedule set before you. You don't have to rush into the shower, get dressed, and snatch a quick cup of coffee as you race out the door to face the day's work. As a matter of fact, there is no work. No alarm, no rush-hour traffic, and no grueling 8-hour routine. You don't have to worry about the bills because there are no bills. And forget about keeping up with the Joneses because there are no Joneses either. Life is good.

This is Eden, the garden of God. This is the way it was in the beginning.

Now imagine that you've been teleported there, and you wander off to go meet Adam and Eve. You're going to tell them of all the wonderful things that the 21st century has developed, all the witty little devices that we've invented, and how fascinating life will be in the far-off future. Of course, you will discreetly leave out the war, disease, crime, and immorality because that will only spoil the picture that you want to paint for them.

When you get past telling them about the advances of technology and begin to describe what a typical day is like, you notice that the expression on their faces has changed from wonder to disillusionment. A description of our society and the things that drive and influence it brings an even darker reaction from them.

This may not be what you expected, but it sure isn't what they expected either.

Life is elementally different than what it was in the beginning. It's not just the physical trappings of society that have changed so much – if that's all it was, it would be called progress – but it's our fundamental values, the core of our society's soul. We have changed and adapted to the lifestyles that we've created, and we don't notice how much we have changed from the original way things were created to be. If we do notice, it is all too easy to dismiss the simplicity of Eden as boring, even naïve, while we tout the excesses of today as exciting and stimulating.

But Adam might have seen us differently. He would have seen us as being trapped inside a hard shell where we have insulated ourselves from God's ways and have created our own humanistic environment. He would probably wonder how we can stand it.

But this is not the way life was designed to be – it is how we made it.

Toward the end of the Book of Deuteronomy, after reviewing the laws of the covenant that God made with them, Moses makes the point that the law of God's righteousness is not something that should seem strange or different from the natural. He notes that it isn't something hidden from us here on Earth or that is only natural in Heaven and has to be brought down and imposed on us. Neither is it something so hidden and mystical that you have to search to the ends of the world to finally discover Truth.

No, the righteousness of God "…is very nigh unto thee, in thy mouth, and in thy heart, that thou mayest do it" (Deut. 30:14). In other words, it is the most natural thing in the world, and it should be as easy as sliding into an old shoe.

But that natural ease is no longer found in our world today. It's a lot easier to fall into sin than it is to fall into righteousness, because our world is poised to scintillate the lust, passions, and pride of our flesh, not the righteousness of God.

A trace of that old Holy Ghost conviction is still in us, however -- that is, until we harden our consciences through sin. But we are a clever race, so to counteract that, we have the innate imagination to create religions that will cater to whatever style we would like and soothe that nagging conviction that still echoes in the depths of our hearts. Of course, all these "belief systems" are great to live by -- I just wouldn't want to die by them.

That's why we need a Savior. Not a figurehead for our church, but a personal Savior who is able to not only change our hearts but also provide a means for us to walk right in His Spirit every day. Only through Salvation can we ever get back to that original, natural walk with God.

Church alone can't do it; government for sure can't do it; our family might try, but they can't do it either. Education only serves to stimulate the mind, but it can't change our hearts. Doing charitable works may make us think we've earned it, but this is not something we can earn.

No, there is a wall that separates us from that natural place of righteousness in God. We can't climb over it, but there is a doorway provided for us so that we can walk through to the other side and escape this old world of sin.

That Door is Jesus Christ.

Four Bucks

I'd like to share with you a letter I got last week that shows the incredible value of a small sacrifice.

While I was in Kenya, I purchased Bibles in the Swahili language to give out to those who needed them. I've learned three things about giving Bibles:

1. If you're going to go broke buying Bibles, that's a good way to go broke.
2. If you spend the money, God will pay you back. (And even if He doesn't, so what!)
3. It is impossible to know the extent of what a Bible placed in the hands of a hungry heart can do.

It is hard for us in America to grasp the depth of poverty in many other nations, but in almost every place I have visited, the cost of a simple Bible is too expensive for most common people. Bibles are precious to them, but the extra money to afford one is scarce.

Here are a few short excerpts out of a letter that was written by someone who received one of those Bibles. I'm sure it will touch your heart:

"Dear Brother,

"I live in Nairobi where you once visited. I was in the church the first time you came. You may not remember me because I was always quiet, and I am not so much known there.

"...I feel very much pushed in my heart to thank you for what you did to me. I know you are wondering, 'What!', but brother, God bless you, you gave me a Bible!!

"I am so grateful about this, and I thank God for your visit to Kenya. You became a blessing to me. It is the Bible that I use now, and I know God will reward you for this. You bought Swahili Bibles for the Makadara Fellowship and I happened to receive one. Thank you so much, God bless you. As I read it, I always remember you and thank God for you and your family...

"...We shall connect again if it is God's will. Remember, the Bible you gave me changed my life completely. It is the most precious gift I have ever received since I was born.

"God bless you."

Four bucks – that's all it cost – just four bucks for a Bible. And look what four bucks has done in the life of a girl halfway around the world.

Her letter is five pages long, full of glowing praise for God and the fire of the Holy Spirit that is inside her. Her life has truly been transformed, and there is no telling how many other lives she will also touch because of it.

Americans are, without a doubt, the most generous people on Earth, but sometimes we don't know where to give or who to help. The next time you drop into the local convenience store and drop a few bucks down for some incidentals, think of what that could mean in the life of someone who is desperate for the Truth, and ask God to open an opportunity for you to give. He may be waiting for that one prayer from you so that He can direct you to give someone else a miracle that will change his or her life.

Four bucks – that's all that Bible cost. But how do you put a value on what four bucks can do? For this girl, and those who will be touched by her, it is worth more than all the riches this world could ever offer.

I believe I will get to meet this girl in Heaven someday, and I have a feeling that she'll be standing there clutching that same Bible that she received that day so long ago in a little church halfway around the world.

Four bucks – that's all it cost, but it brought the life-changing transformation of Salvation to a soul who will spend Eternity with Jesus because of it.

> *"Cast thy bread upon the waters: for thou shalt find it after many days. Give a portion to seven, and also to eight; for thou knowest not what evil shall be upon the earth." Ecclesiastes 11: 1-2*

Changed

"And I, if I be lifted up from the earth, will draw all men unto me." John12:32

A friend of mine once said that a Christian's idea of a party is to get a case of Coke, sit around, and talk about death. Pretty strange, huh? Everybody loves to have a good time – Christians are just focused on the later rather than the now.

While we may choose to celebrate our Savior's birth, we are commanded to celebrate His death because that is what has set us free. No other religion or belief system has that same focus. We're so different from everybody else that even the Lord calls us "peculiar." It's not that we're weird – it's just that Salvation has transformed us so completely that we have become new creatures in Christ.

To have that change occur in us, however, we must follow Jesus to the Cross, where we pick up our own cross and allow our old nature to die through repentance and surrender to God. That's a mouthful but suffice it to say we have to die to have life.

But if that was all there was to it, then it would not go any further than that, and we would experience a meaningless death. While the Cross is the center-post of all Eternity, it is His resurrection that gives us hope. We are saved by the blood of Jesus, but we enter into new life through His resurrection. Things are now different: we have a new path in life, a new purpose, and a brand-new goal.

So, we celebrate death with our new life. Is it a small wonder that those who are unsaved and who have never experienced the wonders of Salvation have trouble understanding us?

Have you ever had a terrific experience and tried to tell your friends all about it? While you're fumbling around for the right words to explain it so they can understand, they just sit there dumbly looking at you with expressionless eyes. "(Yawn) Oh, that's nice." That's what it is like trying to explain how wonderful it is to finally be in the Spirit of God and have Life.

So, the next time you meet someone with that excitement in their eyes and that glow on their face as they try to tell you about Jesus Christ, their Savior, and how you should get saved, instead of dismissing them as if they are just overblown with zealous fervor, maybe you should wonder what it is that they have that you don't.

When you step through the Door of Salvation, you enter into another world that, although it may take you down some rough roads, ultimately leads to

Life. You no longer are focused on what this world can offer you because you have something better. You are no longer eager for carnal blessings, prosperity, or riches in this life because your treasure is in Heaven, and you are not worried about what others think of you. You were just like them once upon a time, but now you are changed and are on the road to Glory.

Like you, they will never understand until they experience it for themselves.

> *"But the natural man receiveth not the things of the Spirit of God: for they are foolishness unto him: neither can he know them, because they are spiritually discerned… but we have the mind of Christ."* *1st Corinthians 2:14*

> *"Wherein they think it strange that ye run not with them to the same excess of riot, speaking evil of you"* *1st Peter 4:4*

> *"But ye are a chosen generation, a royal priesthood, an holy nation, a peculiar people; that ye should shew forth the praises of him who hath called you out of darkness into his marvelous light"* *2nd Peter 2:9*

Somebody get the Coke. Let's have a party!

Chesed

I was reading my daily chapter of Proverbs today and came across a scripture that stopped me in my tracks:

Proverbs 19:22 – "The desire of a man is his kindness: and a poor man is better than a liar."

I don't think I've ever really understood that proverb. What is "his kindness"? And what has that got to do with being a liar? I had to look it up.

"Kindness" is the Hebrew word, *"chesed,"* which has to do with lovingkindness toward something or someone, but it goes much farther than that. It is most often used as God's *"chesed"* toward man or Israel. It is one of the most important words in the Old Testament.

It is not a loving favor based on a covenant or an agreement, nor is it dependent upon anything reciprocal. It is part of God's nature that He expresses His love toward man through his *"chesed."* God's desire is not that mankind should spend Eternity in Hell or be rebellious and thereby receive the curses of judgment. We are the focus of His *"chesed."*

The covenants, even the death of His Son, are all a result of God's *"chesed"* toward mankind, even to the infinite wisdom of His Plan that Paul exclaims so loudly as being past understanding.

So, a man's desire, then, is his "*chesed*." It is his heart's focus, the object of the vision that he has in his heart. Like God, it is not dependent upon anything reciprocal, or being repaid, or even being fair. It just is.

For some people, their "*chesed*" may be unborn children sacrificed to abortion. To others, it may be their family, their church, lost souls, or whatever thing or purpose your heart yearns for. I honestly believe that it is God who places that "*chesed*" in every man's heart that drives us in our personal quests in life and gives us a sense of purpose and direction. He has engineered us all so that we all have different purposes in the Body.

Okay. I get that so far, but what does that have to do with being a liar?

Again, I looked it up and found that the word "*kazav*" does mean to lie, to be found untrue or faithless, and often appears with the word for "vanity" or "emptiness." False witnesses and false prophets are guilty of "*kazav*" because it encompasses the sense of violating a holy trust by claiming that the thing that God is testifying as true is actually a lie. It's more than just a lie. It is the violating of a sacred trust, either to ourselves, to God, or to our *"chesed."*

Now, it's coming together.

So, in a sense, when we have a *"chesed"* that has been placed in us as a deeply embedded desire of our hearts, it becomes a sacred trust to ourselves. If we violate that holy trust by denying it or not following that vision, it would be better for us to have nothing at all. When God gives you a vision, follow it. It is the destiny of your life. It is your "chesed."

Taking it one level higher: when you accept Jesus Christ as your personal Savior, God plants the *"chesed"* of the Great Commission on you. It is not something learned; it is embedded in the Christian's heart when you get saved. It is part of the transformation that accompanies being "born again." It is our "first love" (Rev. 2:4). It is our *"chesed."* To neglect that vision by sitting in church all your life and not acting upon the commission that God has placed upon you would, in essence, cause you to be a liar to something that is the essence of your calling in God -- a violation of your Christianity. It would be your *"kasav."*

The perfect example is in the parable of the Talents in Matt. 25 and Luke 19. You are given a talent. Do not hide it in the ground or wrap it in a napkin. Many of you have hidden dreams away in your heart that you long to follow but have been kept back because of the things of Life that have gotten in the way. Your "chesed" has become so buried behind so many obstacles that it may seem impossible to resurrect it to the forefront of your life again.

I say, follow your dreams and let God work out the details. Don't die with an unfulfilled dream in your heart. It was placed there by God for a reason to be your destiny. To deny it would be akin to violating a trust with your own personal purpose for life.

God threw everything to the wind to send down His very heart in the person of His only begotten Son to follow His "chesed" toward Mankind. He asks us to do the same.

Stupid Eve

> *"And the woman said unto the serpent, We may eat of the fruit of the trees of the garden: but of the fruit of the tree which is in the midst of the garden, God hath said, Ye shall not eat of it, neither shall ye touch it, lest ye die.*
>
> *And the serpent said unto the woman, Ye shall not surely die: for God doth know that in the day ye eat thereof, then your eyes shall be opened, and ye shall be as gods, knowing good and evil."* Genesis 3:2

A funny thing struck me about this scripture this morning: God didn't tell them anything about touching the tree – He just said don't eat of it (Gen. 2:17). Why did Eve add that little quip? Could it be that she was bugged that God had put restrictions on her freedom, so she added that as a kind of snotty comment?

Maybe, maybe not. Still, she did wonder why she wasn't allowed to partake in that wonderful tree that was right there in the middle of the garden. It was a beautiful tree. And just look at that good-looking fruit! What on earth was so wrong with it?

To top all that, if they could eat of that fruit, they would become wise. Now, c'mon, what's wrong with that? Doesn't God want us to be wise? How could that possibly be a bad thing? Or is that the wrong kind of wisdom and knowledge?

You know, if God really didn't want us to eat of that tree, then why didn't He place it somewhere out of sight, like out on the outskirts of the Garden? Oh no, He had to stick it right smack dab in the middle of the Garden, right where we have to pass by it every day. You know, I don't think that was very fair of Him to stick something so good right in front of our faces every day and then tell us He would kill us if we ate it. That's almost like dropping a woman off in the middle of a Shopping Mall with a bunch of money and telling her she can't buy anything.

So how could Satan resolve this conflict? "Umm, let's see, if we tell her that she heard wrong, she'll know we're lying. Let's face it, the commandment was pretty simple. Even an idiot would understand it. So that won't work.

"We can't tell her that God was actually talking to someone else and it didn't really apply to her, because there isn't anybody else around. No, that won't work either.

"Oh! I got it! Let's tell her that even though God really did say that, He really didn't mean it. Let's come from the "God is Love" angle (everybody loves to hear that God loves them), and we'll just convince her that He really wouldn't go through with killing them. Yeah, He said that, but He didn't really mean it.

"Besides, it's not fair that God would withhold such a lovely tree from you. Why is God afraid that you will learn the knowledge of both good and evil? You know, maybe God is afraid that you'll become really smart just like Him, and then He would lose His authority over you. After all, you're pretty smart, aren't you, and you can learn all that theological stuff too. What do you need God for? Who does He think He is to hold you back from being smart? Just a little bit of learning and studying some books, and pretty soon, you can quote all that religious stuff just like Him. We could even come up with some titles for you with little letters after your name. "

When Satan slides in with his flattery and smooth deception, it is easy to fall for it because it can sound like he makes so much sense, and if it is something that you want to be true anyway, it is all too easy to allow yourself to believe his lies.

Stupid Eve. Instead of focusing on what God wanted, she was more interested in what she wanted.

Stupid Adam. Instead of taking a stand against what he knew was wrong, he was afraid he would lose the wife God had given him, and like a weak pastor, he allowed his congregation to rule over him.

I hate to say this, but although this is an old story, it still works today. Satan still tells the same lies, and humanity still falls for them. So many people live their lives the way they want without any regard for the commandments of God but still think they are pretty good people and will go to Heaven anyway.

Satan's job is not to convince you that sin is not sin – no, he knows that won't work. His job is to convince you that you can get away with it. Isn't that what he told Eve? "…Ye shall not surely die" (Gen. 3:4)

You cannot justify sin. You can't say that you will go to Heaven anyway, even though you know you are breaking His commandments – and please don't try the excuse that you said a prayer once upon a time, so you are exempted because He loves you so much. And you can't say that God didn't really mean what He has said, or that the Word of God is just a book written by men, so it doesn't mean anything.

Either you will eat off the Tree of the Knowledge of Good and Evil, or you will eat off the Tree of Life. One tree is focused on what <u>you</u> want in life, while the other requires subjection and humility to focus on what <u>God</u> wants in your life.

You can't have both.

Me and God

I am not a warm, fuzzy emotional type of guy.

I don't know if I've always been that way or if it's just getting more pronounced as I become a crotchety old man. I like things cut and dried. I like Math rather than English, I'd rather puzzle over a Geometry problem than play Scrabble, and I get more of a thrill figuring out how a machine works rather than appreciating Modern Art. (What? You're supposed to *feel* something when you look at it?)

When it comes to the Gospel, I have a better understanding of what God requires from us than of the unimaginable love that He has for us. The specter of Hell has always loomed higher to me than the promise of Heaven. Over time, however, I have learned to just accept the love of God for whatever it is and keep on going. I'll figure it all out later when I get to Heaven.

But I read a poem the other day that stopped me dead in my tracks with a single line of verse, "Jesus died for us because He couldn't bear to live without us."

My first impulse was to dismiss it as some more soppy "love" poetry, but as I paused, it struck me how true it was. He really did love us that much. It's just hard to understand why. As an old preacher once said, "I can understand His judgment, but I'll never understand His mercy." It's far easier for me to grasp His sovereignty and authority over us than this notion of how much He really did care about us.

That led me to think about prayer.

I have always maintained that to be a strong Christian, you must have a strong prayer life, not only in quantity but in intensity. I was taught to storm the Throne of God in prayer until you broke through and that if you wanted an answer in prayer, you could get it, but you had to contend like a warrior until you got that breakthrough.

I still believe that.

Some folks may not understand what that is like. Weak Christianity has inserted the notion of just "having a little talk with Jesus makes it right" for so long that, for some folks, to watch a real prayer warrior at work is a scary thing. They've been taught that it's okay to just sit quietly with your hands folded and hum your way to God. But if you don't know what it is like to battle with strong, contending prayer, then you'll never know what it is like to break through to the Throne of God.

What an exciting experience that is! You pray like a steam locomotive, and then, all of a sudden, the heavens open up, and the Spirit of God crashes down on you in buckets – and you KNOW you got an answer! Believe me, you won't get that if you pray like Mortimer Meek.

On the other hand, the notion of ferocious prayer had been so drilled into me that I guess I felt that if I didn't pray hard, God wouldn't hear me. If I wasn't prepared to pray like Elijah, then I didn't pray at all. Everything had to be so structured and prepared as if I was packing for a long hike up the mountain. As a result, I missed a lot of intimate moments with God – moments when it was just Him and me, and I didn't have to rip down any barriers to get to Him.

But the thought that He actually gave His life because He couldn't bear to live without me just cracked that hard spot in my heart like a sledgehammer. I turned it over and over again in my mind. Wow. That opened up all kinds of new avenues in my understanding.

That means that God not only can hear you, but He is actually listening, waiting for your call.

Now true, the Bible says that "the effectual, fervent prayer of a righteous man availeth much" (James 5:16), and that God is able to do "exceeding abundantly above all that we ask or think" (Eph. 3:20). If you work that power, you will get breakthroughs; if you pray like Elijah, you will get the same results; and if you really want an answer, you may have to fight for it, but that doesn't take away those precious moments of intimate prayer when it is just you and God in the stillness of solitude.

If He gave His life so we could be with Him for all Eternity, how much more does He want to spend these precious, personal moments with us now?

Nice to be Nice

I had a very nice Easter. We visited some relatives and attended church with them on Easter morning, and went to their early "traditional" services. It was wonderful to hear those old-fashioned Gospel songs that have so much depth and feeling in them. It rejoiced my heart to hear them again.

All in all, it was a very nice service, and it was a very nice church, with a very nice pastor who gave a very nice sermon that left us all feeling so very … um … nice. Five minutes later, however, I forgot what it was about, but I'm sure it was very nice.

Now, while it is nice to be nice, and it makes for a comfortable experience on Sunday morning, I have always had a problem with that. I am just not satisfied with "nice." Maybe it's because I got saved in a church that was on fire for God and was immersed in the outpouring of the Holy Ghost in every single service.

I fully expect the power of God to be more than just an idea in the back of my mind. I want to experience the electricity of the Holy Spirit filling the whole room with His presence like a cloud that is so thick that you can cut it with a knife, and I want the message that comes across the pulpit to come straight down from the Throne of God and pierce my heart so that I walk out of that service different than what I was when I walked in.

Am I asking too much?

Sometimes I think I am. After all, these are all really nice people, and they all mean well and want to be good Christians. But other times, I am reminded that God will spew the lukewarm out of His mouth (Rev.3:16) and that He raises up His ministers to be a flame of fire (Heb.1:7), not "nice guys."

Sometimes I think that maybe I'm just too wild and crazy and that it really is okay to be "nice." When I consider what is at stake here, however, and that the difference has eternal consequences, I wonder if it will still be okay 10,000 years from now when we're spending Eternity in one place or the other.

I don't blame the congregations; I blame the ministers. The Bible doesn't say, "Woe to the flocks that scatter the shepherds"; it says, "Woe be unto the pastors that destroy and scatter the sheep of my pasture!" (Jer. 23:1).

Our ministers today are more polished and sophisticated than ever before. They are Ph.D.'s, Th.D.'s, and Rev.'s (and whatever other little letters they can put in front or in back of their names). They have framed diplomas hanging on their office walls and are members of all sorts of theological organizations just to further their sophisticated education. They have been taught all sorts of ways to prepare their messages and sometimes spend all week getting it right so that they can cover their pulpit with well-ordered notes (just in case they forget what the message was).

They have a well-structured form of godliness, but, honestly, I would rather have the power of God.

God does not care how much "stuff" you know, how many degrees you have, or what a nice guy you are. God wants you to surrender and allow Him to take over. After all, it's not about you; it's about Him.

Are you a nice, loving pastor who is worried about offending your congregation, so you are afraid to preach too strong of a message? That is the same mistake Adam made with Eve.

Do you think you will increase your wisdom by reading books or studying theology? The Bible says that wisdom is the Fear of God and the knowledge of the Holy is understanding.

Do you have a nice, complacent church where everyone is comfortable, or are you burning with the fire of God?

Do you spend all week preparing your Sunday message, or are you yielded enough to let the power of the Holy Ghost flow through you and deliver a message straight from the Throne of God? Who's preaching on Sunday? You, or God?

Are souls getting delivered, hearts being changed, and lives being transformed every week, or do you just have "church as usual"?

Is the Blood of Jesus Christ flowing at the altar of repentance, or has the fire on your altar burned down so low that you don't remember the last time someone got saved?

Are you a minister that God has raised up as a flame of fire, or are you just a nice guy?

Yeah, it's nice to be nice, but you know what? I'd rather be on fire.

Two Gospels

There are two Gospels in America. The first is the one we are most familiar with, that God loves us as His people and that America is basically a Christian nation.

Sure, we're going through a bit of a dry time right now, but don't you worry, God is about to pour out His wonderful blessings on us all. Most notably, He will deliver a great transference of wealth upon the Christians. All the prophets of peace and prosperity tell us that this is so.

We are all going to be rich! Isn't that wonderful? Not only that, but God is also going to deliver us out of so many of the troubles that we are going through right now. We just have to have faith and hang on to those beliefs, and of course, show our faith by sending money to the C.C.A.A. (That's Christian Con Artists of America.)

Wow, it sounds so good that it has caught the attention of all those who feel the need right now – which, admittedly, is most of us.

Not only that, but we're going to have a revival! Isn't that nice of God to do that for us? Just pick a city, and there is sure to be some prophet there who has heard from God that it is coming first to a city near you – Dallas, Phoenix, St. Louis, Kansas City, Los Angeles, and a whole litany of others.

Hooray! Let's all get saved and get rich!

I suppose it all makes some kind of sense because this generation has been repeatedly told that God loves us and that He isn't a God to be feared because He is our Daddy.

Gosh, it makes you feel all warm and cuddly inside.

But I'm left sitting here scratching my head because I don't see anything that remotely resembles what the Word of God requires to have such an outpouring of the Holy Spirit. But then, maybe I'm just reading an old version of the Bible.

But we all love something for free, right? So why not believe in a Gospel of entitlement where you don't have to do anything to receive the blessings of God? We can have an easy-going, smooth Gospel that will bring a revival for free, and all we have to do is sing and dance on Sunday morning.

This new Gospel has done away with many of the elements of the old-fashioned one:

Gone are the all-night prayer meetings for God to save souls. When we do pray, it is usually for ourselves and for what we want God to give to us. I call it the "Gimme Gospel."

Gone are the cries for holiness. They have been replaced by the Love Gospel, which calls for "relationships" instead and love for those who are "hurting." But my Bible says without holiness, no man shall see the Lord (Heb. 12:14).

Gone is the anguish in our hearts for the lost that are on their way to Hell. (Oops. Is that a 4-lettered word?) Instead, we have the Nice Gospel which is full of programs to help us be more socially minded.

Gone are the anointed messages of power from our pulpits that came down straight from the Throne of God. Our seminaries have thought up a better way of preparing the message all week with the help of numerous theological study helps. Shucks, you can even order a pre-packaged sermon off the Internet, complete with audio-visual presentations.

Gone are our altars that were once filled with repentant souls desperate for Salvation.

Gone are the abundance of miracles and healings that once flowed so abundantly.

Gone is our heritage of a people that once feared God.

In its place is a coming Judgment that will begin at the House of God.

Psalm 45 – Religion and Faith

"My heart is inditing a good matter..." Psalm 45

As I read Psalm 45, I see that David knew Jesus Christ, the Son of God. That's a little startling when you have been told all your life that the Jews only believed in a single God -- the Father. The very idea of a triune Godhead has been an abomination to their religious doctrine.

But David knew.

Immediately, my mind flipped through the scores of other references to the Messiah throughout Psalms, even referring to him as "the Son" in Psalms 2.

If that isn't enough, perusing through the hundreds of Messianic prophesies paints such an exact picture of Christ that it is a wonder that there is even any question about it. The exact day of Christ's triumphant entry into Jerusalem is lined out in Daniel – the exact day! Even Herod knew He was coming.

But we have been led to believe over the years that Judaism makes no allowance for a "Son" of God. For centuries, Jewish sons and daughters that converted to Christ were disowned and rejected, even to the point of burying an empty casket.

How has this happened? How have a people chosen by God to be His own become so disenfranchised from Him?

I have always believed that they knew and even expected him when he came, but Jesus Christ was not the type of Savior they were looking for. They made a choice, and it was the wrong choice.

There is a difference between religion and faith. Religious knowledge and spiritual understanding see things very differently. It is a dichotomy that has its roots in the difference between the carnal and the spiritual mind. Faith is not established with what we see with our eyes but with what we believe in our hearts.

It has always been this way, and it is the same today. If we make the same mistake that the Jews made, we will find ourselves with the same result. Just because we settle back into complacency because we believe we are the children of God, that does not make it so.

Judaism is a religion. So is Christianity. But faith speaks of something beyond what our eyes see. David's heart was inditing a good matter, not his mind. He saw into another realm that could not be defined by religion or the carnal mind. He was not directed by religious traditions and dogma – he was led by his heart.

If we, as Christians, do not look past our religion, we will not see God. And when He moves in a way we were not expecting, we will miss it, just like they did 2,000 years ago.

There is more to God than just church, but to find it you will have to pull yourself out of this world and reach out with your heart. And when you find it, it won't look anything like religion.

> *"Hearken, O daughter, and consider, and incline thine ear; forget also thine own people, and thy father's house; So shall the king greatly desire thy beauty: for he is they Lord; and worship thou him."* *Psalms 45:10,11*

Bait

> *"And a certain man lame from his mother's womb was carried, whom they laid daily at the gate of the temple which is called Beautiful, to ask alms of them that entered into the temple;*
> *Who seeing Peter and John about to go into the temple asked an alms."*
>
> *Acts 3:2,3*

What a surprise this guy ended up getting!

This guy had been lame all his life and knew the best place to set himself up to get a few shekels out of passersby as they were entering church. He had a regular spot there, and everybody knew who he was, so he must have been doing okay for himself – maybe not great, but at least he knew how to work the crowd.

Then along comes Peter and John. The only problem was that they were broke.

This guy had no idea what was coming. He didn't even know enough to ask for healing, never mind expect one. He was just trying to scrape together enough pennies to eat. But God healed him anyway. I think that was pretty cool.

But the thing that has always stood out to me was how amazed everyone was at this healing. Wasn't it just a few months ago that all of Israel was buzzing with all the miracles that Jesus had done? So why were they so surprised? Did they not believe the stories they had heard?

Or maybe they didn't want to believe them.

You see, if they believed in those miracles, then Jesus had to be the Messiah, and if that was true, that means they killed the Son of God, and if THAT was true, they were in a hell of a lot of trouble! It would be a whole lot easier to just turn off the switch, ignore the stories, and make believe it never happened.

After all, where was Jesus now? Dead gods never impress anybody -- miracles or no miracles -- and Jesus was dead (wasn't He?).

It's the same today. Yeah, we remember the stories about the Brush Arbor revivals, the Faith Healers like Aimee Semple McPherson, Katherine Kuhlmann, Smith Wigglesworth, and so many others, but where are they today? They're all dead! When was the last time you saw the blind to see, lame to walk, and deaf to hear? Been a while, has it?

We don't believe it anymore because we have not seen a flowing of the miraculous working power of God in years. There's a reason why that is -- we're not hungry enough. Until we become desperate, we will remain in the belly of an apostate slump. As long as we're satisfied with complacency and are not cut to the heart for what we are missing in God, then we will sit right there waiting for a revival that will never come. God will not set His seal of approval on an apostate church that doesn't care.

Want to know how to get God to move? Simple. God hears desperate prayer, and He feeds desperate hunger, and we're just not desperate enough. The blueprint for revival in the Book of Joel calls for fasting, and weeping, and mourning. What kind of prayer is he calling for? To howl! Rend your hearts! Lie all night long before the altar and cry unto the Lord! That's the kind of prayer God is calling for, and we are just not there yet.

Ask any fisherman – you can take your very best rod and reel with the most expensive bait out to the ol' fishing hole, position yourself perfectly and fish there all day long … but if the fish ain't hungry, they won't take the bait.

And we ain't hungry.

Approved

"Oh, there's trouble!
Right here in River City!
With a capital 'T', and that rhymes with 'P', and that stands for Pool!"

("The Music Man" by Meredith Wilson)

The Apostle Paul had more than his share of trouble with the Corinthians. Like a bunch of zealous baby Christians who were still carrying a lot of baggage from their pagan traditions, he had to deal with a constant stream of issues that needed to be resolved. Some were serious; others were not, but they all had to be dealt with.

It was of primary importance to establish a firm bedrock that the developing church would be built upon. The path that the church would take for hundreds of years would be set in those early days, and every little divergence from the Truth would be magnified down the road. Paul had to set the church firmly on the correct path from the very beginning, or it would end up either destroyed or at best, marginalized.

His warning to them is chilling:

> *"For there must be also heresies among you , that they which are approved may be made manifest among you."*

There is not a church in existence that Satan does not have a plan of attack for. He knows the weaknesses and strengths of everyone there, from the Pastor to those nestled in the last pew, and he has a plan to exploit those weaknesses.

Heresies and divisions will rise up in your church – you can bet on it. It is not a matter of whether these will come or not; it is how you will deal with them and what the reaction will be from the rest of the church when you do.

God will turn Satan's plan around to His own glory, but to do that, He has to use men and women who are yielded to His will. Those who are "approved," as Paul puts it, are those who have allowed God to put them through a refining fire so that they come out stripped of all their own ways and become compliant with the ways of God. These are men and women who answer to God only and who will stand up in defense of the Truth no matter what.

When God raises up these men and women as a standard against the enemy, mark them. They may cause discomfort; they may be abrasive; they may not be concerned about offending anyone, but they are the ones whom the Lord will make manifest among you to establish and purify your church.

If your church hearkens to those whom the Lord raises up, it will be healed, but if the church does not, then it will choose a path that will end up in complacency and will lose the vision that God had purposed for it.

Whether you are the pastor or the doorkeeper, hearken to the reproof of those whom the Lord has approved. It is the way of Life.

> *For the commandment is a lamp; and the law is light; and reproofs of instruction are the way of life: (Proverbs 6:23)*

Artificial Death

"In the way of righteousness is life; and in the pathway thereof there is no death." **Proverbs 12:28**

This is one of those scriptures you can read a hundred times and pass over it every time, but it is a scripture that strikes at the most important issue of the entire Bible – Life and Death.

"In the way of righteousness is life…" What does that really mean?

Obviously, there is no encapsulating edict that keeps Christians from suffering trouble, sickness, or death. Everybody experiences hard times, and everybody that breathes has life … sort of. So, what is this "life" that righteousness brings us that is so different from that which the world gives?

The difference between those two different kinds of life is what is at the very heart of the Gospel.

If the Gospel of Jesus Christ were just another philosophy, then this scripture would be meaningless. We would experience nothing different than what sinners do. We would feel the same, breathe the same, sense the same things, and put our pants on the same way. The only difference between us would be in our cognitive beliefs about religion.

And, of course, both of us would think the other was wrong.

But the Gospel is not a philosophy about religion – it is the power of God unto Salvation that completely transforms a human soul into a brand-new creature in God (Rom. 1:16). There's a palpable difference that can be felt all the way down to the depths of your being when you get saved. It is the great difference between those who are in the Spirit of God and those who are not. It is a feeling so tangible that for thousands of years, real Christians have been willing to sacrifice everything they had, including their lives, in defense of the Cross.

It is difficult to describe what that kind of "life" is like in tangible terms. Jesus said that it was like the wind – you can't see it, but you can sure feel it (John 3:8). That's why it is so difficult for someone who has had little else than basic religion to understand what this scripture is really describing.

But – ah yes, but! -- once you have experienced the life-changing transformation that happens to you when you get saved, you never forget it. You then know what real life is for the first time in your life. If you understand that Sin kills the soul, and only the Blood of Jesus Christ can wash that sin away and give life, then it is easy to see that religion is little more than another philosophy and cannot give life – it is

Salvation that brings a transformation in your soul that is likened to being born again into a brand-new life.

What about the rest of the Scripture? How can there be no death in the pathway of righteousness? Do we not all die? How can this scripture possibly be correct if everybody dies?

No, death is artificial. The soul never dies -- you just change clothes when you cross over into the next life. Now, it might be said that you will WISH you were dead if you die in your sins, but you won't die. Ten thousand years from now, you will be somewhere – either in Heaven or in Hell – but you will be very much alive (if you can call it that).

What if you have gone to church all your life, but you have no understanding of what this scripture is talking about? You have never felt any different than the next guy, but you've maintained your belief that you are going to Heaven because you believe in God, and you show up for church every week. You're a good guy, but you've never felt the power of God rip you from death into life.

Maybe you've missed something along the way; maybe "church" isn't enough. Maybe just believing that God is up there somewhere without ever having actually met Him has relegated Him to little more than just a religious concept in your head. If that is so, then your idea of "life" is confined to nothing more than a muscle pumping in your chest while your soul is dying with sin.

If death is artificial, then it might be time to find out what life is.

> *"Verily, verily, I say unto thee, Except a man be born of water and of the Spirit, he cannot enter into the kingdom of God. That which is born of the flesh is flesh; and that which is born of the Spirit is spirit. Marvel not that I said unto thee, Ye must be born again."* ***John 3:5-7***

Trust the Lord

"The Horse is prepared against the day of battle: but safety is of the Lord"
Proverbs 21:31

"Dad, you're working too hard. You need to trust the Lord."

This is what a son of a friend of mine told him the other day. I asked him what he was going to do, and he replied, "Well, I'm going to trust the Lord, of course."

Okay. That sounds good. And just what exactly does that mean? Is there a switch somewhere that has to be turned on? How do we do that – "just trust the Lord"? I'll bet all of us have said this very same thing – we're going to trust the Lord – but it never occurs to us what plan of action we will follow to bring that about. We're just going to do it … somehow.

I believe that you must come to a predetermined place in God before you can have that level of trust where you are absolutely sure that God will reciprocate in kind. If you decide to go ahead and step off the edge of a cliff, just muttering a phrase about trusting the Lord may not be enough to break your fall.

There must be more of a reciprocal relationship with God to be absolutely sure that He will catch you when you step off the precipice. Anything less than that is not faith or trust – it is presumption, and, to some degree, tempting the Lord. Even Jesus refused to jump off the pinnacle of the Temple when tempted by the devil, even though it had been written in black and white in the Word of God that the Messiah wouldn't dash his foot against a stone.

The "Name it, and Claim it" crowd might disagree, but the Bible says that the kingdom of God is not in "word" but in "power" (1 Cor. 4:20). There has to be more than just a verbal statement to put substance in your faith.

Trust is a form of surrender. It is the letting go of your fleshly ways, thoughts, and works so that you may give yourself over to a crucified walk in the Spirit of God, completely yielded to His Will, so that you can allow God to take complete control of the reins of your life, no matter what.

That's a mouthful! And how do you bring yourself to a place of surrender like that? How do you come to a place of brokenness where you have given up on your own ways and have totally given yourself over to the Will of God? The world (and the worldly churches) will tell you that you don't have to come to a place of such abject submission, and you don't have to go through the sufferings of the Body of Christ because Jesus did it all for you on the Cross. Well, good luck with that Gospel, but it doesn't line up with the Bible that I read.

No, we are commanded to deny ourselves, pick up our cross, and follow Him (Matt. 16:24). In that broken, crucified walk, we find ourselves in a place of complete surrender to God's eternal will. Whatever He has for us, whether it be good or bad, we are willing to give ourselves over to it because the whole of God's Plan is greater than our individual parts. Jesus died to save souls, and He asks us to do the same.

When you get to a place in God where you are given over to His Will, you know that whatever happens, you are in the hands of God. That's the definition of trust.

So back to the original question: how do you get there?

Not to oversimplify things, but really, it comes down to reading and prayer. Seek the face of God like your life depends upon it -- that's where your power comes from to walk in His Spirit. If you forget your reading and prayer, you can forget your power in God.

Do bad things happen to Christians? Of course, but when you are no longer part of this world, it doesn't matter because you are in Him and the sufferings of this world fade in the face of His glory. If you are dead to this world, nothing matters anymore.

Only then can you step off the edge of the cliff and trust that His hands are right there to catch you.

> *"In the world, ye shall have tribulation: but be of good cheer; I have overcome the world."* John 16:33

Peter Fishing

> *"Simon Peter saith unto them, I go a fishing. They say unto him, We also go with thee. They went forth, and entered into a ship immediately; and that night they caught nothing." John 21:3*

Jesus had told his disciples that when he died and rose again that they were supposed to go to the mountain in Galilee. The angel at the tomb told them the same thing. Did they go? No, they hung around Jerusalem instead.

Cowering in a room for fear of the Jews, they waited because they just didn't know what else to do. Their Savior and Master had been crucified, and although they had been told over and over again, they still had a hard time believing that Jesus would rise from the dead. He had to appear in person before them for them to really believe.

Did they go, then? Nope. Eight days later, Jesus had to show up again and rebuke Thomas about their unbelief.

Okay, now they got it, and off to Galilee they went.

But when was Jesus supposed to show up? The Bible doesn't say how long they waited in the mountain that they were supposed to go to, but after a while, they finally decided to go fishing themselves. Without Jesus.

It has often been said that waiting is the hardest thing for a Christian to learn to do. Waiting on the Lord requires real faith -- not that you believe God is up there, but that God is totally in charge. There is an issue of broken humility here that is needed for us to overcome our own ways, ignore the things that we want to do, and toss out our schedule of when we want God to do what we think He should do and when we think He should do it. We give God a timetable and an agenda, and when we don't see God move for us, then we rush off to take care of business ourselves. Much like Saul when he decided to make a sacrifice without waiting for the prophet Samuel as he was instructed. That didn't work out too well, either.

When we rush off in presumption, we preempt the work of God and take upon ourselves the authority that belongs to God alone.

And then we wonder why we didn't catch any fish.

So, when Jesus showed up at the prearranged place, there was no one there to meet Him. No, they were out in the boat doing their own works. And they got predictable results.

Peter knew he was wrong. He was naked, exposed, without a covering for his presumptuousness, and threw himself into the sea. It was better than facing his foolishness.

One of the greatest mistakes of many Christians is to attempt to do the works of God without Him. It is also one of Satan's most effective traps. We rush off in the name of the Lord to build new churches, establish great works, and precipitate great moves of God … all in vain.

The cart doesn't pull the horse; the horse pulls the cart.

We think we are simply showing our faith in God, but all we are doing is exercising our presumption. But presumption is not faith – it is sin. We think we are doing this for the kingdom of God, but really, we are only doing this for ourselves. Charity requires being broken to God's leading and timing so that the Spirit of God is accomplishing to work, not human flesh.

Paul admonished Timothy about the results of running ahead of the Lord:

> *"Now the end of the commandment is charity out of a pure heart, and of a good conscience, and of faith unfeigned: from which some having swerved have turned aside unto vain jangling; desiring to be*

teachers of the law; understanding neither what they say, nor whereof they affirm." 1Timothy 1:5-7

Wait on the Lord. Pray, fast, and seek His face, but if you really believe Him, then wait. If you don't get an answer when you thought you should have, then pray some more. But wait upon the Lord.

The works of flesh never yield results in the Spirit.

Ezekiel and the Prophets

> *"And her prophets have daubed them with untempered mortar, seeing vanity, and divining lies unto them, saying, Thus saith the Lord GOD, when the LORD hath not spoken."* Ezekiel 22:28

It sounds like the people in Ezekiel's day had the same kind of prophets that we have today.

And ol' Zeke had the unenviable job of exposing them for what they really were. No one likes to hear that his precious beliefs are wrong, but what else was Ezekiel supposed to do? Just grin and bear it when God was breathing fire down his neck?

I wonder if you could hear a sigh come out of Ezekiel every time he got a word from the Lord, knowing that he would be hated for the things that God had commanded him to say. Let's face it, it's a lot easier to hate someone who is telling you to repent than it is to hate God for making him tell you, so Ezekiel had to know that he was going to catch the brunt of the people's ill will.

It's a tough job being a real prophet because their whole purpose in life is to tell you the very thing that you don't want to hear. The false prophets have it easy – they get all the praise and accolades for making everyone feel good. I'll bet they get plenty of tithes too. Maybe that's why they choose to mollify their messages with all that warm and fuzzy stuff about how we're such "fair-haired boys" in God's eyes. Like good salesmen, they only tell you what they know you want to hear.

There are thousands of them out there, running around like gypsy fortune-tellers, telling people all sorts of wonderful, encouraging words to make them feel good. Like "Home on the Range," there is seldom a discouraging word to be heard.

And as a result, there is no repentance. And therefore, no forgiveness.

Neither is there any persecution. (At least not for them.)

Today, we even have schools that will teach you how to be a prophet. Boy, does that sound cool! Just think, for a hundred bucks, you can be the first on your block to be a prophet of God! I wonder if you can get a diploma to hang on your wall next to your staff so everyone knows that you've been certified.

I always tell young people who think they've been called to be a prophet to hurry up and ask God if they can get their money back. Maybe you can make God change His mind before it's too late because to be a real prophet of God, not only will you die a thousand deaths before you get there, but nobody's going to like you very much when you do.

But then, maybe I'm just old-fashioned. Maybe all you have to do is stick your hand in the air and go with whatever puff of wind happens to come along. If it feels good, just say it!

Yeah, the old-time prophets had it tough. Their job was to stand in the gaps and declare unto the people of God their sins and transgressions and call them back to God through brokenhearted repentance. That's why there are so few of them (the real ones, that is).

Most people will follow their hearts, but a wise man loves reproof.

> *"The words of wise men are heard in quiet more than the cry of him that ruleth among fools." Ecclesiastes 9:17*

Oxen

"Where no oxen are, the crib is clean: but much increase is by the strength of the ox." Proverbs 14:4

Work. Ugh! Don't you just love it?

You cannot escape work. We try all sorts of ways to get around it, but we never escape it. It is one of the "blessings" that came out of the Garden of Eden, and it has dogged our tracks ever since.

It is no different with church.

Oxen are dirty animals. You have to clean them, feed them, and even build a crib for them to stay in. And good luck trying to potty-train them. Guess who has to shovel up all their stuff that they leave you.

There is a way to escape all that work, however – get rid of the oxen. That way, the crib stays clean, and you can relax ... which is what you wanted in the first place, right? Relax and cruise through life. Ahh, the peaceful life!

But if you want an increase, if you want your crops to grow, and if you want to eat, then you need those oxen to pull the plow… and that means work.

No church will ever grow without the strength of its pastor. He is the ox that pulls the plow. If your ox is weak and lethargic, you won't get much plowing done. If the ox is taken up with other things that are much more fascinating than those boring, straight rows of dirt, you will end up with crooked rows that run in every direction other than the one you need to get the field done. No, the ox has to work and work hard, otherwise, there will be no harvest.

But just having oxen doesn't constitute a harvest. You can't just stick him in the crib, go back to relax on the porch, and expect bushels of wheat to drop out of the sky. Sorry, it doesn't work like that. You have to get out there and work with him.

I hear so many Christians complain about how hard it is to find a good church. They complain that wherever they go, services are dead, and they feel like they are just going through the motions. They are hard-pressed to find a soul-winning church where the power of the Spirit of God can be felt rather than mimicked.

And forget about miracles of healing and prayer! Instead of the power of God, all they find are carnal celebrations to pump up emotional highs. It feels good, and it's lots of fun, but it's not what they are looking for. They want the real thing. We used to have it, but we lost it somewhere along the line.

And so, we blame the churches and their pastors for what we feel is missing. "Woe to the pastors that scatter the flocks," we say. We complain that the oxen don't have the strength and the drive to do the work. True, a weak message will never produce a strong congregation, but aren't we still just trying to get out of work? If we want a strong church, then we must have a strong ox, but when you get a strong ox, that means you will have to get out there in the field and work as hard as the ox does.

Oops.

Isn't there an easier way? Can't we just get the oxen to do all the work while we sit back and enjoy the benefits of a strong, powerful church? Can't we just hitch the oxen up to the plow and let them run around the field by themselves?

No, you must put your hand to the plow. The plow has two handles -- you put your hand to one handle while God puts his hand on the other handle, and you drive those oxen in a straight line if you want your crops to grow.

And who goes out there after the field is plowed to plant the seed? Not the oxen – they're back in the crib. And who does the weeding? And the watering? And the reaping? Is Jesus supposed to do all that for you? Jesus said that He would separate the wheat from the chaff, but you have to bring the harvest into the threshing floor so He can.

The oxen will work if you work them. People that want a strong, soul-winning church will gravitate to a pastor who will deliver a strong message, but a strong ox cannot do it by himself. It is up to you to work the plow.

Don't complain about the pastor if you're not willing to clean the crib.

> *"And Jesus said unto him, No man, having put his hand to the plough, and looking back, is fit for the kingdom of God."* Luke 9:62

About the Author

Dalen Garris has been in ministry since 1970 during the Jesus Movement in California. In 1997, he began a radio broadcast that ultimately spread to dozens of countries, from Israel and Saudi Arabia to Africa and the Philippines. His program, *Fire in the Hole,* was selected for broadcast four times a week for several years across North America on the Sky Angel network as the Voice of Jerusalem.

A newspaper column followed, for which he has written over 700 articles, which have been published in local newspapers and Christian magazines in several countries. He has also written over a dozen books and several booklets.

Since 2004, he has been lighting the fires of revival in churches spread across sub-Saharan Africa. During the course of 17 years, he has preached in over 1,000 churches and has seen hundreds of them set on fire and explode with growth, and hundreds of new ones planted across Africa. Hundreds of people have been supernaturally healed during the healing lines that so often sprang up during these revival meetings, and tens of thousands have been saved. And the fires are still burning.

Because of his work across Africa, Dalen Garris was awarded an honorary Doctorate in 2017 by the Northwestern Christian University of Florida.

Dr. Garris currently lives with Cindy, his wife of 43 years, in Waxahachie and is still heavily involved with churches across Africa. His pressing hope is in seeing this powerful move of God in Africa ignite us here in America. He believes that this upcoming generation will be the Gideon Generation that will usher in this last, great revival that he has preached about for so many years.

If you would like Dalen Garris to speak at your church or organization, please contact us for times and schedules.

Books by Dalen Garris:

Available at: ***www.Revivalfre.org/books***

Four Steps to Revival

Do You Have Eternal Security?

Standing in the Gap

Two Covenants

Fire in the Hole

Revival Campaigns

The Kenya Diaries

A Trumpet in Nigeria

A Scent of Rain

Into the Heart of Darkness

Fire and Rain

Revival Campaigns in Africa – 2019

The Battle for Nigeria

A Light in the Bush

A Match in Dry Grass

Planting a Seed in Liberia

A Whisper in the Wind

Talking With the Women, by Cindy

A Voice in the Wilderness series:

vol. 1, The Journey Begins

vol. 2, the Early Years

vol. 3, Prophet Rising

vol. 4, Revival in the Wings

vol. 5, Sound of an Abundance of Rain

vol. 6, Watchman, What of the Night?

vol. 7, Mud and Heroes

vol. 8, Ashes in the Morning

vol. 9, Shaking the Olive Tree

vol. 10, Winds of Change

vol. 11, A Final Call

vol. 12, Superficial Shells

Booklets

Available at: ***www.Revivalfire.org/booklets/***

A Volcano in Cape Verde

Tanzania, 2011

Nigeria, 2012

Calvinism Critiqued

When is the Rapture?

RevivalFire Ministries

PO Box 822, Waxahachie, TX 75168

dale@revivalfire.org

www.Revivalfire.org

www.ingramcontent.com/pod-product-compliance
Lightning Source LLC
LaVergne TN
LVHW050639100826
845148LV00011B/1906